Frommer's®

Washington, D.C.
day BY day®

3rd Edition

by Meredith Pratt

D1531147

WILEY
John Wiley & Sons, Inc.

Contents

Published by:

John Wiley & Sons, Inc.

111 River St.
Hoboken, NJ 07030-5774

ISBN 978-1-118-28861-0 (paper); 978-1-118-33386-0 (ebk); 978-1-118-33494-2 (ebk); 978-1-118-33166-8 (ebk)

Editor: Andrea Kahn
Production Editor: Jana M. Stefanciosa
Photo Editor: Alden Gewirtz
Cover Photo Editor: Richard Fox
Cartographer: Elizabeth Puhl
Production by Wiley Indianapolis Composition Services

For information on our other products and services or to obtain technical support, please contact our Customer Care Department within the U.S. at 877/762-2974, outside the U.S. at 317/572-3993 or fax 317/572-4002.

Wiley also publishes its books in a variety of electronic formats. Some content that appears in print may not be available in electronic formats.

Manufactured in China

5   4   3   2   1

A Note from the Editorial Director

Organizing your time. That's what this guide is all about.

Other guides give you long lists of things to see and do and then expect you to fit the pieces together. The Day by Day guides are different. These guides tell you the best of everything, and then they show you how to see it *in the smartest, most time-efficient way*. Our authors have designed detailed itineraries organized by time, neighborhood, or special interest. And each tour comes with a bulleted map that takes you from stop to stop.

Hoping to relive the glory days of Washington and Jefferson, visit Butterstick (the baby panda) at the National Zoo, or tour the Smithsonian Institution's free museums? Planning a walk through Georgetown, or dinner and drinks where you can rub shoulders with lawmakers and other D.C. celebrities? Whatever your interest or schedule, the Day by Days give you the smartest routes to follow. Not only do we take you to the top attractions, hotels, and restaurants, but we also help you access those special moments that locals get to experience—those "finds" that turn tourists into travelers.

The Day by Days are also your top choice if you're looking for one complete guide for all your travel needs. The best hotels and restaurants for every budget, the greatest shopping values, the wildest nightlife—it's all here.

Why should you trust our judgment? Because our authors personally visit each place they write about. They're an independent lot who say what they think and would never include places they wouldn't recommend to their best friends. They're also open to suggestions from readers. If you'd like to contact them, please send your comments our way at feedback@frommers.com, and we'll pass them on.

Enjoy your Day by Day guide—the most helpful travel companion you can buy. And have the trip of a lifetime.

Warm regards,

Kelly Regan

Kelly Regan, Editorial Director
Frommer's Travel Guides

About the Author

A Baltimore native and a Washingtonian for more than 10 years, **Meredith Pratt** is an avid traveler, writer, and art lover. Her work has profiled international travel locales, high-powered personalities, and top D.C. destinations. Pratt's writing has appeared in *USA Today, Executive Travel, Baltimore Magazine, WebMD*, the *Magazine, Washington Flyer*, and many others.

Acknowledgments

To Adam, for always keeping me grounded. And to my family, whose constant encouragement and support has been there when I needed it most. Thousands of thanks to my wonderful friends, who help make every day worth it.

Advisory & Disclaimer

Travel information can change quickly and unexpectedly, and we strongly advise you to confirm important details locally before traveling, including information on visas, health and safety, traffic and transport, accommodations, shopping, and eating out. We also encourage you to stay alert while traveling and to remain aware of your surroundings. Avoid civil disturbances, and keep a close eye on cameras, purses, wallets, and other valuables.

While we have endeavored to ensure that the information contained within this guide is accurate and up-to-date at the time of publication, we make no representations or warranties with respect to the accuracy or completeness of the contents of this work and specifically disclaim all warranties, including without limitation warranties of fitness for a particular purpose. We accept no responsibility or liability for any inaccuracy or errors or omissions, or for any inconvenience, loss, damage, costs, or expenses of any nature whatsoever incurred or suffered by anyone as a result of any advice or information contained in this guide.

The inclusion of a company, organization, or website in this guide as a service provider and/or potential source of further information does not mean that we endorse them or the information they provide. Be aware that information provided through some websites may be unreliable and can change without notice. Neither the publisher nor author shall be liable for any damages arising herefrom.

Star Ratings, Icons & Abbreviations

Every hotel, restaurant, and attraction listing in this guide has been ranked for quality, value, service, amenities, and special features using a star-rating system. Hotels, restaurants, attractions, shopping, and nightlife are rated on a scale of zero stars (recommended) to three stars (exceptional). In addition to the **star-rating system,** we also use a **kids icon** to point out the best bets for families. Within each tour, we recommend cafes, bars, or restaurants where you can take a break. Each of these stops appears in a shaded box marked with a coffee-cup-shaped bullet .

The following **abbreviations** are used for credit cards:

AE	American Express	DISC	Discover	V	Visa
DC	Diners Club	MC	MasterCard		

Frommers.com

Now that you have this guidebook to help you plan a great trip, visit our website at **www.frommers.com** for additional travel information on more than 4,000 destinations. We update features regularly to give you instant access to the most current trip-planning information available. At Frommers.com, you'll find scoops on the best airfares, lodging rates, and car-rental bargains. You can even book your travel online through our reliable travel booking partners. Other popular features include:

- Online updates of our most popular guidebooks
- Vacation sweepstakes and contest giveaways
- Newsletters highlighting the hottest travel trends
- Podcasts, interactive maps, and up-to-the-minute events listings
- Opinionated blog entries by Arthur Frommer himself
- Online travel message boards with featured travel discussions

A Note on Prices

In the "Take a Break" and "Best Bets" sections of this book, we have used a system of dollar signs to show a range of costs for 1 night in a hotel (the price of a double-occupancy room) or the cost of an entree at a restaurant. Use the following table to decipher the dollar signs:

Cost	Hotels	Restaurants
$	under $100	under $10
$$	$100–$200	$10–$20
$$$	$200–$300	$20–$30
$$$$	$300–$400	$30–$40
$$$$$	over $400	over $40

An Invitation to the Reader

In researching this book, we discovered many wonderful places—hotels, restaurants, shops, and more. We're sure you'll find others. Please tell us about them, so we can share the information with your fellow travelers in upcoming editions. If you were disappointed with a recommendation, we'd love to know that, too. Please write to:

Frommer's Washington, D.C. Day by Day, 3rd Edition
John Wiley & Sons, Inc. • 111 River St. • Hoboken, NJ 07030-5774
frommersbeedback@wiley.com

12 Favorite
Moments

12 Favorite **Moments**

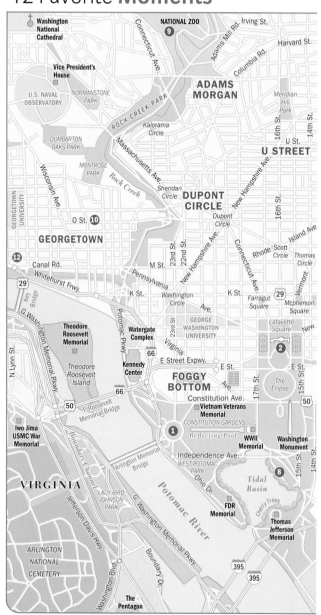

Washington
National
Cathedral

NATIONAL ZOO
❾

Irving St.

Adams Mill Rd.

Harvard St.

Columbia Rd.

Connecticut Ave.

**Vice President's
House**

**ADAMS
MORGAN**

Meridian
Hill
Park

*NORMANSTONE
PARK*

16th St.

14th St.

*U.S. NAVAL
OBSERVATORY*

ROCK CREEK PARK

U St.

U STREET

Kalorama
Circle

*DUMBARTON
OAKS PARK*

Massachusetts Ave.

New Hampshire Ave.

16th St.

Rock Creek

*MONTROSE
PARK*

Sheridan
Circle

**DUPONT
CIRCLE**

GEORGETOWN
UNIVERSITY

Wisconsin Ave.

Dupont
Circle

Island Ave.

O St. ❿

23rd St.

22nd St.

New Hampshire Ave.

Connecticut Ave.

Rhode
Scott
Circle

Thomas
Circle

GEORGETOWN

M St.

Vermont

❶❷

Canal Rd.

Pennsylvania

Mcpherson
Square

Whitehurst Frwy.

29

Key
Bridge

K St.

Washington
Circle

K St.

Ave.

29

Farragut
Square

G. Washington Memorial Pkwy.

N Lynn St.

Potomac Pkwy.

**Watergate
Complex**

23rd St.

Virginia

**GEORGE
WASHINGTON
UNIVERSITY**

Lafayette
Square

New

**Theodore
Roosevelt
Memorial**

66

**Kennedy
Center**

E Street Expwy.

E St.

❷

*Theodore
Roosevelt
Island*

66

**FOGGY
BOTTOM**

Ave.

E St.

17th St.

*The
Ellipse*

E St.

15th St.

50

T-Roosevelt Memorial Bridge

Constitution Ave.

**Vietnam Veterans
Memorial**

50

**Iwo Jima
USMC War
Memorial**

Arlington Memorial Bridge

CONSTITUTION GARDENS

Reflecting Pool

**WWII
Memorial**

**Washington
Monument**

15th St.

14th St.

❶

Independence Ave.

VIRGINIA

Boundary Channel

*LADY BIRD
JOHNSON
PARK*

*WEST POTOMAC
PARK*

Ohio Dr.

*Tidal
Basin*

❽

Jefferson Davis Hwy.

Potomac River

Cherry Trees

*ARLINGTON
NATIONAL
CEMETERY*

Washington Blvd.

Boundary Dr.

**FDR
Memorial**

**Thomas
Jefferson
Memorial**

G. Washington Memorial Pkwy.

395

395

The Pentagon

Previous page: The U.S. Capitol in spring.

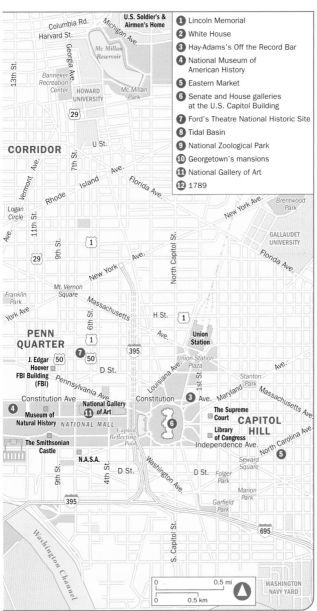

1. Lincoln Memorial
2. White House
3. Hay-Adams's Off the Record Bar
4. National Museum of American History
5. Eastern Market
6. Senate and House galleries at the U.S. Capitol Building
7. Ford's Theatre National Historic Site
8. Tidal Basin
9. National Zoological Park
10. Georgetown's mansions
11. National Gallery of Art
12. 1789

President Harry Truman famously once said: "If you want a friend in Washington, get a dog." While it's true that the city is known for its passionate politics, presidential scandals, spies, and more, American politics, with its Hollywood-like allure, is not the only attraction drawing a never-ending stream of visitors to the nation's capital. It's a city of stunning architecture. World-class museums. Zeitgeist-changing theater. Cherry trees and great green spaces. Historic neighborhoods. Super shopping. An international pool of locals who call this place home. And, of course, the monuments that honor the brave, the fallen, and the founders of this fine country. Washington is inevitably targeted for laughs, but once you arrive in D.C., you'll be smiling, too.

❶ Stand at the foot of the Lincoln Memorial and gaze across the National Mall. The view—of the Reflecting Pool, the Vietnam and World War II memorials, the Washington Monument, and, in the distance, the Capitol Building—is monumental. *See p 9.*

❷ Peer through the iron fence at 1600 Pennsylvania Avenue for a glimpse of America's most famous residence. Unless you reserved a tour months in advance, you can't get close, but the vision alone is enough to renew your patriotic spirit. *See p 31.*

❸ Eavesdrop on the hushed conversations between D.C. movers and shakers at the Hay-Adams's venerable Off the Record Bar.

Grab a stool and chat with longtime bartender John Boswell, confidant to ambassadors, spy masters, and presidents. Then cross Lafayette Park, past the White House, to the POV Bar in the W Hotel for sweeping, not-to-be-missed views of the National Mall. *See p 151.*

❹ Marvel at the country's cultural and historic icons at the Smithsonian's National Museum of American History. This sprawling spot is home to the Star-Spangled Banner, Dorothy's ruby slippers, Kermit the Frog, and more. *See p 68.*

❺ Troll for treasures from Eastern Market on Capitol Hill. Savor a piping hot coffee and flaky pastry as you scavenge for secondhand baubles, retro clothing, colorful flowers,

The Reflecting Pool on the National Mall, with a view to the Washington Monument.

The White House.

organic fruits and vegetables, and one-of-a-kind arts and crafts. *See p 101.*

6 **Observe elected officials at work during a session of Congress.** Or watch the American legal system in action, just a few blocks away, at the United States Supreme Court. *See p 29.*

7 **Take in a show at the reno-vated Ford's Theatre.** The historic site is a living memorial to President Abraham Lincoln, who was assassi-nated there in 1865. Along with an exhibit of collected artifacts, the theater hosts some of the most cel-ebrated plays from Lincoln's period. *See p 56.*

8 **Stroll along the Tidal Basin.** This small reservoir adjacent to the Potomac River becomes a sea of blossoming pink flowers in March and April. Pose for a photo in front of the Jefferson Memorial or grab a paddle boat and hit the water in warmer months. *See p 126.*

9 **Roar right along with the lions, tigers, and bears at the**

Eastern Market.

Think Pink

D.C. is another world in late March and April, when its ubiquitous Japanese cherry trees, a gift from the city of Tokyo in 1912, burst into bloom. Even politicians lose their pallor amid the clouds of pink flowers along the Tidal Basin. The **National Cherry Blossom Festival** (☎ **844/44-BLOOM** [442-5666]; www.nationalcherry blossomfestival.org) includes a crew race, fireworks, a dinner cruise, a Japanese street fair, and more.

National Zoo. Then visit the famous giant pandas and elephant house. And don't miss the petting zoo or the nearby "pizza" playground for very young children. *See p 48.*

🔟 **Bask in history amid Georgetown's massive mansions.** Most are at least 100 years old; many were built several centuries ago. In Georgian and Federal styles, they bear grand architectural details—such as round rooms and circular central staircases—that have all but disappeared from modern structures. *See p 90.*

⓫ **Wander the marble halls of the National Gallery of Art.** From Rothko to Rembrandt, the museum showcases some of the very best art and sculpture in the city. Take in traditional works in the West building, then head to I. M. Pei's East Wing for more contemporary classics. *See p 60.*

⓬ **Romance your significant other over a prime bottle of wine at 1789.** The crackling fire and soft lighting at this tony New American restaurant has warded off many a chill on a Georgetown evening. *See p 141.* ●

Joggers on the National Mall.

1 The Best **Full-Day Tours**

The Best of D.C. in **One Day**

1 Lincoln Memorial
2 Vietnam Veterans Memorial
3 Washington Monument
4 National World War II Memorial
5 Korean War Veterans Memorial
6 Martin Luther King, Jr. Memorial
7 FDR Memorial
8 Jefferson Memorial
9 Pavilion Café
10 National Gallery of Art
11 National Museum of American History
12 The Source
13 Off the Record Bar

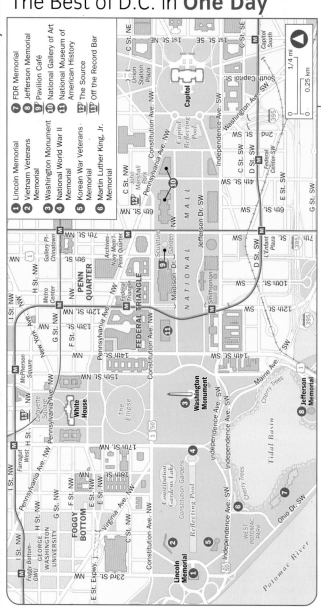

Previous page: The Library of Congress.

This full-day tour guides you through the Mall and Georgetown, the two parts of the District you must explore before leaving town, despite the fact that Georgetown is slightly off the public transportation grid. Both attract visitors in droves for good reason, so don't feel like a lemming if you end up trailing kids in matching T-shirts as you explore the Mall's free monuments and museums and the cobblestone sidewalks of M Street in Georgetown.

START: **Metro to Foggy Bottom, then a 30-minute walk**

Travel Tip

I recommend exploring D.C. on foot, but those who can't might consider **D.C. Tours** (☎ 888-878-9870; www.dctours.us). Its red, white, and blue double-decker sightseeing buses travel around the city and allow you to hop on or off at various stops. Buses leave every 20–30 minutes. One fare is good for the day ($30 for passengers 16 and up; $15 for kids 5–15; free for under 5). National Park Service rangers are on duty at the following monuments daily 9:30am–11:30pm. The **National Mall Shuttle** (☎ 202/289-1995; www.graylinedc.com) runs in a loop from Union Station to the World War II Memorial, and around many historical Mall sites. The cost is $5 per boarding.

❶ ★★★ Lincoln Memorial. Start your day on the steps of this iconic tribute to Abraham Lincoln, the beloved 16th president of the United States. Architect Henry Bacon designed this marble, Greek temple–inspired memorial in 1914. Its 36 Doric columns reflect the states of the Union at the time of Lincoln's assassination in 1865—days after the Southern states surrendered in the Civil War. Daniel Chester French designed the nearly 20-foot-tall (6m) sculpture of Lincoln, seated in solemn repose, surrounded by inscriptions of his immortal words from the Gettysburg address and his second inaugural address. You'll likely feel chills while gazing across the Mall and contemplating Lincoln's "dedication to the proposition that all men are created equal." ⏱ 30 min. ☎ 202/426-6841. www.nps.gov/linc. Free admission. Metro: See start, above.

❷ ★★★ Vietnam Veterans Memorial. In Constitution Gardens, "The Wall" honors the 58,000 servicemen and -women who perished or disappeared during the Vietnam War. Two black slabs of granite seem to grow from the earth toward each other, joining to form a wide "V." Designed in 1980 by Maya Ying Lin, then an undergraduate at Yale, it has been likened to a "scar in the earth," evoking the deep rift the war created among Americans. The

The Lincoln Memorial.

The Vietnam Veterans Memorial.

names of the dead and missing are inscribed in the reflective stone. In reverent silence, mourning families make rubbings and leave flowers for their late sons, daughters, brothers, sisters, husbands, and wives. 🕐 *20 min.* ☎ *202/426-6841. www.nps. gov/vive. Free admission. Metro: Foggy Bottom, then a 25-min. walk.*

③ Washington Monument. Robert Mills designed this 555-foot-tall (169m) monument to honor

The Washington Monument.

President George Washington. The world's tallest masonry structure when it was built in 1884, it's visible from points throughout the city. The monument itself and its observatory, with its breathtaking views of the city, closed due to damage caused by the August 2011 earthquake and are not scheduled to reopen until late 2013. 🕐 *20 min.* ☎ *202/426-6841. www.nps.gov/ wamo. Free admission. Metro: Smithsonian, then a 10-min. walk.*

④ National World War II Memorial. After controversy between activists demanding a tribute to "the greatest generation" that fought and died in World War II, and naysayers who didn't want the Mall altered, this serene memorial was completed in 2004—without obstructing the views of the Lincoln Memorial or Washington Monument. Built of bronze and granite, it features 56 pillars that represent the unity of the states and territories in their decision to enter the war. The 4,000 sculpted gold stars on the Freedom Wall signify the

400,000 Americans who died fighting between 1941 and 1945. 🕐 *20 min.* 📞 *202/619-7222. www.nps. gov/nwwm. Free admission. Metro: Farragut West, Federal Triangle, or Smithsonian, with a 25-min. walk.*

⑤ Korean War Veterans Memorial.

This representation of 19 larger-than-life ground soldiers slogging through a field, dressed in identical flowing rain capes, helmets, and battle gear, is haunting. Completed in 1986, it reminds viewers of a war forgotten by many, and honors the men and women who gave their lives for it. 🕐 *20 min.* 📞 *202/426-6841. www.nps.gov/ kowa. Free admission. Metro: Foggy Bottom, then a 30-min. walk.*

⑥ Martin Luther King, Jr. Memorial.

This relatively new monument, completed in August 2011, is a tribute to the Civil Rights leader who made his famous "I Have a Dream" speech on the steps of the Lincoln Memorial in 1963. A 30-foot-tall (9m) relief of King called the "Stone of Hope" is found just past two other pieces of granite known as the "Mountain of Despair," a visual metaphor for the struggles King encountered during his lifetime. 🕐 *20 min.* 📞 *202/426-6841. www.nps.gov/mlkm. Free admission. Metro: Smithsonian, then a 20-min. walk.*

⑦ FDR Memorial.

This 7½-acre (3-hectare) outdoor memorial with four outdoor rooms, or galleries, celebrates the man who saw the U.S. through the Great Depression and much of World War II. Designed by Lawrence Halprin in 1978 (and completed in 1997), it tells the story of Franklin Delano Roosevelt's four-term presidency: Each gallery represents the challenges of the time and showcases FDR's most famous quotes alongside sculptures of soup lines, the president in his wheelchair, his passionately political wife Eleanor, and more. 🕐 *20 min.* 📞 *202/426-6841. www.nps.gov/ frde. Free admission. Metro: Smithsonian, then a 30-min. walk.*

⑧ ★★★ Jefferson Memorial.

Modeled after the Pantheon in Rome, this circular colonnaded structure fronts the picturesque Tidal Basin—which is lined with cherry trees that burst into rosy color from late March through mid-April. Architect John Russell drew from Thomas Jefferson's love of neoclassical design to celebrate the third president's contributions as a scientist, architect, politician, musician, diplomat, and inventor. Dedicated in 1943, it features a 19-foot-tall (5.7m) bronze statue of Jefferson inside. 🕐 *20 min.* 📞 *202/426-6841. www. nps.gov/thje. Free admission. Metro: Smithsonian, then a 25-min. walk.*

The Korean War Veterans Memorial.

It's tough to know where to find a quick bite to eat amid so many museums and government buildings. The 9 kids **Pavilion Café**, in the National Gallery of Art Sculpture Garden, has a solid menu of salads, sandwiches, espresso drinks, and baked goods. Dine outdoors on warm days, or gaze out at the ice-skating rink in winter. *9th St. and Constitution Ave. NW.* ⏱ *45 min.* ☎ *202/289-3360. $. Metro: Archives, Judiciary Square, or Smithsonian.*

⑩ ★★★ **National Gallery of Art.** If you visit only one of the city's free art museums, make it this one. Founded in 1937, the museum has a permanent collection that spans 9 centuries of masterworks: early Italian and Flemish Renaissance paintings, including the single Leonardo da Vinci painting in the U.S.; the High Renaissance works of Titian; the Dutch interiors of Vermeer; the pre-Impressionist and Impressionist works of Monet, Manet, van Gogh, Degas, Toulouse-Lautrec, Gauguin, and Cézanne; and the modern masterpieces of Picasso, O'Keeffe,

Johns, and Pollock, to name a few. Art lovers may want to reserve a whole day to wander these halls. Everyone else should allot 2 hours. ⏱ *2 hr. See p 60 for service details.*

⑪ ★★ **National Museum of American History.** Want to see the original Kermit the Frog hand puppet? How about Dorothy's ruby red slippers, Archie Bunker's chair, or Muhammad Ali's boxing gloves? America's history is told through its objects, art, advertising, communications, and popular culture at this beloved museum. The Star-Spangled Banner, the flag that inspired the national anthem, has been recently restored and is now housed in a dramatic new gallery and atrium dedicated to its preservation. Julia Child's kitchen; a 1903 Winton (the first car driven across the United States); and 14 dresses from First Ladies including Laura Bush, Jackie Kennedy, and Michelle Obama are just a few more of the objects

Edgar Degas' Little Dancer Aged 14, at the National Gallery.

The Washington Skyline

As you wander among the monuments, memorials, and museums, you can't help but notice the **U.S. Capitol Building** (see p 28) at the eastern end of the Mall; the **Federal Reserve Building** on Constitution Avenue, almost directly across from the Vietnam Veterans Memorial; and the **White House,** behind its imposing wrought-iron fence, at 1600 Pennsylvania Ave. The new **Capitol Visitors Center** (p 28) features an exhibit hall and detailed tour information. The **White House Visitor Center,** at 15th and E streets, offers more details and a 30-minute video. See "Political Washington" on p 28 for more information.

The Capitol Building.

on display here. If you wish to spend an afternoon or a full day here, see the museum tour in chapter 3. ⏱ *1 hr. See p 68.*

After touring the Mall, head just north to the Newseum, where you'll find **12** **The Source,** the sleek, glass-walled restaurant of celebrity chef Wolfgang Puck. An American menu with an Asian twist features sushi, Chinese duckling, and American seafood and steak. *See p 141.*

No visit to D.C. would be complete without a stop at the legendary drinking establishment **13** **Off the Record Bar** in the historic Hay-Adams Hotel, across Lafayette Park from the White House. The bar is a favorite place to see and be seen in the District and a haunt of journalists, lobbyists, politicians, and statesmen—some of whom just might be pictured in the dozens of political caricatures on display. *See p 151.*

Muhammad Ali's boxing gloves, at the National Museum of American History.

The Best of D.C. in **Two Days**

1 National Zoological Park
2 National Archives
3 Eastern Market
4 Library of Congress
5 U.S. Capitol Building
6 Supreme Court
7 The Mall
8 Sonoma Restaurant and Wine Bar
9 Shakespeare Theatre

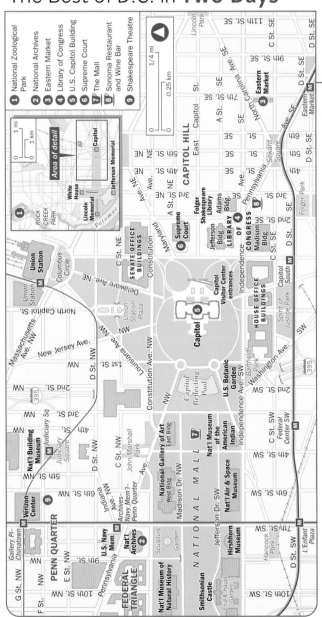

Begin your second day at the National Zoo—home to giant pandas, lions, tigers, elephants, and other rare species. If you set out early enough (the zoo grounds open at 8:30am), you'll have time left to explore Capitol Hill—from the bustle of Eastern Market to the hustle of lawmakers and judges in the U.S. Capitol and Supreme Court buildings, both open for tours and spectators. START: **Metro to Woodley Park–Zoo**

① ★★★ **kids** **National Zoological Park.** The giant pandas are the main attraction at this 163-acre (66-hectare) park in downtown D.C. You won't need tickets to catch a glimpse of any of these rare creatures, but crowds regularly flock to see the pandas romp through their enclosure and eat frozen treats, so be sure to get there early if seeing the bears is a priority. Established in 1889, the National Zoo is home to some 500 species, many of them rare and/or endangered. You'll see cheetahs, zebras, camels, gorillas, hippos, seals, monkeys, meerkats, and, of course, lions, tigers, and (other) bears. If you have very young children, the hilly terrain can be tiring, especially on hot days. The zoo rents strollers, and the Kids' Farm provides a nice break from all that walking. Children 3 to 8 can observe farm animals up close: ducks, chickens, goats, cows, and

The Panda House, at the National Zoo.

miniature donkeys. 🕐 *60–90 min. Start: 8:30am and allow 20 min. for Metro to next tour stop. 3001 Connecticut Ave. NW, adjacent to Rock Creek Park.* ☎ *202/633-4888. www. nationalzoo.si.edu. Free admission. Daily Apr–Oct (weather permitting):*

Big cats at the National Zoo.

grounds 8:30am–7pm; animal buildings 10am–6pm. Daily Nov-Mar grounds 8:30am–7pm; animal buildings 10am–4:30pm. Metro: Woodley Park–Zoo/Adams Morgan or Cleveland Park.

Need a quick coffee or snack? Look for one of the three year-round eateries on zoo grounds: the **Mane Restaurant** on Lion/Tiger Hill, **Panda Café** near the Giant Panda Habitat, or **Panda Plaza Grill** near the Panda Gift Shop. **PopStop**, across from the Small Mammal House, is seasonal. Vending machines are positioned near restroom and information facilities throughout the park.

2 ★★ National Archives. After the Zoo, return to the Metro and head for the National Mall where you'll find, among the Smithsonian museums, some of the most important historical documents in U.S. history. The original Declaration of Independence, signed by members of Congress; the Constitution; the Bill of Rights; and other fascinating glimpses into America's past are on display in the Rotunda of the National Archives Building. The

Emancipation Proclamation, Articles of Confederation, Edison's light bulb patent, and letters from Abraham Lincoln can also be ogled at in this monument to history. ⏱ 1 hr: Start 10am. One-hour guided tours are available Mon–Fri 9:45am. Reservations for self-guided tours are encouraged. 700 Pennsylvania Ave. NW. www.archives.gov. Mar 15 to Labor Day Mon–Fri 10am–7pm; Day after Labor Day to Mar 14 Mon–Fri 10am–5:30pm. Closed Thanksgiving and Dec 25. Metro: Archives/Navy Memorial.

3 ★★ Eastern Market. Built in 1873, this city institution is a flea market, farmer's market, and crafts fair all rolled into one. Recharge over lattes, pancakes, muffins, omelets, or even ham sandwiches and salt-and-vinegar chips here before you shop. The outdoor lot fills on weekends (Mar–Dec) with farmers and fresh produce, artisans and ceramics, and bargain-hunters haggling over a mishmash of antiques. ⏱ 1 hr. See p 101 for service details.

4 Library of Congress. Want to see the original "rough draft" of the Declaration of Independence written in Thomas Jefferson's own

The original Declaration of Independence, at the National Archives.

The Reading Room at the Library of Congress.

hand? This American treasure is here, along with the papers of other presidents, historic maps, revolving exhibitions, and multimedia resources. Created in 1800, the small library was burned by the British in 1814 during their infamous siege on Washington, but it was quickly re-established once Jefferson donated his personal collection of books and artifacts. ⏲ *1 hr.; arrive 30 min. before tour begins. Docent-led, scheduled public tours depart Mon–Sat, in the Great Hall of the Thomas Jefferson Building, at 10:30, 11:30am; 1:30, 2:30, and 3:30pm. No 3:30pm tour on Sat. 1st St. SE (btw. Independence Ave. and E. Capitol St). www.loc.gov. Mon–Sat 8:30am–4:30pm, except for federal holidays. Metro: Capitol South or Union Station.*

⑤ ★★★ **U.S. Capitol Building.** This majestic, 19th-century neoclassical landmark has served as the seat of American lawmaking since the first Congress in 1800. In 1793, George Washington laid the cornerstone of Dr. William Thornton's original design, and various architects saw to the building's completion in 1819. A museum of American art and history, as well as its principal civic forum, the Capitol is worth a stop just to see its architecture and hundreds of paintings, sculptures, and other artworks throughout its 17-acre (6.8-hectare) floor area. Tours can be arranged at the new Capitol Visitor Center (☎ 202/226-8000; Mon–Sat 8:30am–4:30pm except Thanksgiving, Dec 25, and Jan 1), whose exhibition hall features the original plaster cast of the *Statue of Freedom,* the bronze statue that stands atop the Capitol dome, as well as 24 sculptures from the Capitol's Statuary Hall depicting each state's favorite sons and daughters. Visiting the CVC and the Capitol are free, and you can pre-order Capitol tour tickets online. All food, beverages, large bags, and pointed objects are prohibited. ⏲ *1 hr. Entrance at the Capitol Visitor Center on E. Capitol St. at 1st St. NW.* ☎ *202/226-8000. www.visitthecapitol.gov. Metro: Capitol South or Union Station.*

Tip

You can find complete coverage of how to view the House or Senate galleries in session in "Political Washington" (see p 28).

⑥ ★★ **Supreme Court.** The chamber of the U.S. Supreme Court, the highest tribunal in the land, has been restored to its mid-19th-century appearance. Its nine justices, appointed for life terms, decide our collective fate—whether they're weighing in on federal laws or, more rarely, sealing a contested presidential election. The Court convenes the first Monday in October and stays in session until it has heard all its cases and handed down decisions. The Court hears oral arguments the first 2 weeks of each month on Monday, Tuesday, and Wednesday. Visitors can listen to the arguments on short tours, or they can watch the day's entire proceedings. 🕐 *1–2 hr.; lines can be long, so be prepared to wait for up to 1 hr. If you're a legal eagle or Court TV fanatic and absolutely must see the day's full proceedings, arrive by 8:30am and get in line early, for first-come, first-served seating. Everyone else can start at 2pm or 3pm and gain entry with time to spare. 1st St. NE (btw. E. Capitol St. and Maryland Ave. NE).* ☎ *202/ 479-3211. www.supremecourtus.gov. Free admission. Mon–Fri 9am– 4:30pm, except for federal holidays. Metro: Capitol South or Union Station.*

You have an hour or two before dinner and don't want to spoil it. If the weather is warm, grab a soda and snack at any of the many vendor carts stationed on the **7 Mall**. Then, either relax on the grass and people-watch, stroll and admire the sights, check out a monument, or

take in one of the dozens of events held on the Mall through the year— from kite-flying festivals to international dance performances. (Visit www.nps.gov/mall for a schedule.) Otherwise, take shelter at **Union Station** (Columbus Circle at Massachusetts Ave. and 1st St. NE), just a few blocks north, where you'll find snacks, coffee, shopping, and stunning architecture—plus the Metro, for transportation to your next stop.

Oenophiles and fans of simply prepared, New American fare will adore **8 ★ Sonoma Restaurant and Wine Bar**. With 40-plus wines by the glass, plus a lovingly edited wine list of some 200 Italian and French bottles, this upscale but casual bistro is the perfect place to sit and unwind after a long day of sightseeing. Airy and elegant, Sonoma serves "small plates" in four food groupings: cheeses and charcuterie, handmade pasta and pizzas, wood-grilled meats and fish, and organic salads and produce. Book your table in advance to be guaranteed an evening at this ever-popular hot spot. Tip: If you plan to see a show after dinner, make an early reservation and tell your

The Supreme Court.

Sports on the Mall.

server what time you need the check. *223 Pennsylvania Ave. SE.* ☎ *202/544-8088. www.sonomadc. com. Lunch Mon–Fri; dinner daily. Metro: Capitol South.*

⑨ ★★ Shakespeare Theatre. Catch the Bard's best, from *A Midsummer's Night's Dream* to *Othello*, in productions with astounding sets and nationally known actors. Just steps from the Verizon Center, this state-of-the-art theater doesn't have a bad seat in the house, and often features Shakespeare with a twist, such as an all-male cast or modern costumes. *450 7th St. NW (btw. D and E sts.).* ☎ *202/547-1122. www. shakespearedc.org. Tickets $23–$68. Metro: Gallery Place/Chinatown or Archives/Navy Memorial.*

At Sonoma Restaurant and Wine Bar, more than 40 vintages are offered by the glass.

The Best of D.C. in **Three Days**

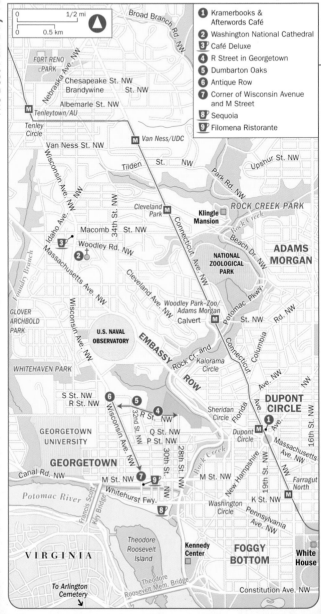

0	1/2 mi	
0	0.5 km	

1 Kramerbooks & Afterwords Café
2 Washington National Cathedral
3 Café Deluxe
4 R Street in Georgetown
5 Dumbarton Oaks
6 Antique Row
7 Corner of Wisconsin Avenue and M Street
8 Sequoia
9 Filomena Ristorante

On your third day, leave the downtown crowds behind and explore Dupont Circle and the National Cathedral. Then spend a leisurely afternoon browsing, spending some dosh, and sipping espressos in Georgetown. By the end of the day, you'll feel as though you know Washington—and chances are you won't want to leave. START: **Metro to Dupont Circle**

1 ★★ **Kramerbooks & Afterwords Café.** This bookstore, grill, and coffee shop is the nerve center of Dupont Circle. A legendary gathering place, it's always packed with cool college kids, stylish gay men, voracious readers, debating politicians, and curious tourists who feel the urge to pick up a copy of Walt Whitman's *Leaves of Grass*. Open early in the morning and late at night, it's the perfect spot to start the day, over breakfast and the *Washington Post*. ⏱ *1 hr. Start: 8:30am. 1517 Connecticut Ave. NW (btw. Dupont Circle and Q St.). ☎ 202/387-3825. www.kramers.com. Breakfast $6.25–$9.75; lunch $8.25–$13; dinner $11–$18. Daily 7:30am–1am. Metro: See start, above.*

2 ★★★ **Washington National Cathedral.** This glorious cathedral, the world's sixth largest, is where presidents are eulogized and sometimes interred, and where many a member of high society is wed. With

Kramerbooks & Afterwords Café, in Dupont Circle.

vaulted ceilings and rich stone carvings, the English Gothic architecture incorporates stones from shrines and historic buildings around the universe. That's right: A piece of lunar rock from the Apollo XI mission is embedded in the stained-glass Space Window. It's a big hit with kids, as is

Dumbarton Oaks.

the Darth Vader gargoyle hidden among the spires. Episcopalian, the church has no local congregation; rather, it has functioned as a national house of prayer for those of various denominations, including Jewish and Serbian Orthodox citizens. (Download your own self-guided tour at www.cathedral.org.) 🕐 *1 hr. Start: 11am. Massachusetts and Wisconsin aves. NW.* ☎ *202/537-6200. Suggested donation $10 for adults and $5 for children and seniors. Mon–Fri 10am–5:30pm; Sat 10am–4:30pm; Sun 8am–6:30pm. Metro to Tenleytown/AU, then take any 30 series bus (31, 32, 36, or 37) going south on Wisconsin Ave.*

Airy and bright, **3** ★★ **kids** **Café Deluxe** is a bustling neighborhood bistro that serves New American classics such as roasted chicken, tuna steaks, and burgers. With small portions and crayons for kids, this is a favorite among families. *See p 136.*

In pleasant weather, walkers will enjoy the roughly 20-minute downhill stroll to R Street, the next tour stop. Everyone else can take the no. 31, 32, 36, or 37 bus lines in front of the Russian Embassy at 2650 Wisconsin Ave. NW, about a block north of the

Washington National Cathedral.

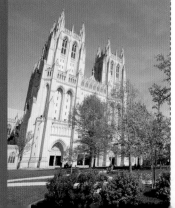

intersection of Wisconsin and Calvert. Taxis are also plentiful on this main drag.

④ R Street in Georgetown.
With its four- and five-story brick Federal- and Georgian-style mansions, its private gardens rife with red tulips and pale pink hydrangeas, and its uniform row houses and manicured lawns, this street epitomizes residential Georgetown. Simply put, R Street between Wisconsin Avenue and 28th Street NW is where most Washingtonians would choose to live if money were no object. It is also home to a spectacular botanical garden; a historic park; meandering trails with romantic benches and weeping willow trees; and a grand, peaceful cemetery. 🕐 *2 hr. Metro to Tenleytown/AU, then take any 30 series bus (31, 32, 36, or 37) going south on Wisconsin Ave.*

⑤ Dumbarton Oaks. Once a private residence, this 19th-century mansion is a research center for studies in Byzantine and pre-Columbian art and history, as well as landscape architecture. A former cow pasture, the grounds of Dumbarton Oaks were fashioned into staggeringly beautiful traditional European gardens—with an orangery and crocus, scilla, narcissus, magnolia, and cherry blossoms. Walkways are lined with bubbling fountains, stone archways, romantic hideaways, tiled pools, and a Roman-style amphitheater. The gardens remain open year-round, weather permitting (Apr–May are peak months). 🕐 *30 min. 1703 32nd St. NW (garden entrance at 31st and R sts.).* ☎ *202/339-6401. www.doaks.org. Gardens: $8 adults; $5 kids and seniors. Tues–Sun year-round; Mar 15–Oct 31 2–6pm, Nov 1–Mar 14 2–5pm (except national holidays and Dec 24). Metro to Tenleytown/AU, then take any 30 series bus (31, 32, 36, or 37) going south on Wisconsin Ave.*

The Samuel Francis Dupont Memorial.

6 Antique Row. Depending on which way you're walking, Antique Row is either a cool cruise downhill or a steep uphill climb. In either case, antiques lovers won't care—they'll be too busy gaping at storefront displays of mint condition 18th-century divans, beautifully painted Persian consoles, weathered ceramic water jugs, and all sorts of one-of-a-kind finds. The best of the lot: Carling Nichols, Blair House, David Bell, and for early-20th-century fans, Random Harvest. Bring your black Amex card for this shopping stroll—prices are that steep. ⏱ *45 min. Start: 3:45pm. Wisconsin Ave., from S to N sts.*

Metro to Tenleytown/AU, then take any 30 series bus (31, 32, 36, or 37) going south on Wisconsin Ave.

7 ★★ Corner of Wisconsin Avenue and M Street. Look down M Street and you'll spy Intermix, Coach, Lacoste, Sephora, Kate Spade, and the new design district, Cady's Alley. Look up Wisconsin and see Benetton, Ralph Lauren, the Apple Store, Baby Gap, Sugar, Urban Chic, and a slew of antiques stores. It could be an expensive afternoon. When you're all shopped out, walk south, downhill, on Wisconsin Avenue. It will deliver you to Washington Harbour and the Potomac River. ⏱ *1½ hr. Metro to Tenleytown/AU, then take any 30 series bus (31, 32, 36, or 37) going south on Wisconsin Ave.*

Stroll the promenade, gaze at the boats slicing through the waves of the Potomac, and then order a cocktail or a cold beer at **8 Sequoia**— you deserve to sit down and relax. But don't snack: Save room for a great meal back towards M Street. *3000 K St. NW (waterfront).* ☎ *202/944-4200. Cocktails $7–$10. Lunch & dinner daily. Metro: Foggy Bottom.*

An antiques store on Wisconsin Avenue in Georgetown.

Side Trip to Arlington: Paying Respects

Arlington National Cemetery's 612 acres (248 hectares) honors national heroes and more than 260,000 war dead, veterans, and dependents. Many famous Arlington graves bear nothing more than simple markers, such as five-star General John J. Pershing's tomb. Highlights include the **Tomb of the Unknowns,** containing the unidentified remains of service members from World Wars I and II and the Korean War. **Arlington House** (☎ **703/235-1530;** www.nps.gov/arho), built by Martha and George Washington's grandson, George Washington Parke Custis, is a 20-minute walk from the Visitor Center. **Pierre Charles L'Enfant's grave,** near Arlington House, is believed to afford the best view of Washington, the city he designed. Below Arlington House is the **gravesite of John Fitzgerald Kennedy.** Jacqueline Kennedy Onassis rests next to her husband, and Robert Kennedy is buried close by. Arrive close to 8am to contemplate the site quietly. The **Visitor Center** offers a detailed map and restrooms.

Tombstones at Arlington National Cemetery.

Washington Harbour has loads of restaurants, but nothing beats 🍵 ★★ **Filomena Ristorante,** a funky Italian restaurant a short walk from the waterfront. The interior is adorned with tacky decorations, doilies, and a zany assortment of seasonal items, but the wine list is great and so is the traditional Italian feel, right down to the cook rolling handmade pasta upstairs. The bowls of handmade pasta are recommended for those who want a true Italian meal. It's casual enough that you won't need to dress up for dinner, but elegant enough that you shouldn't wear shorts. Come hungry: Portions are nearly enough for two. Book your table in advance, especially on weekend nights. *See p 138.* ●

Political Washington

1. U.S. Capitol Building
2. Supreme Court
3. Bullfeathers
4. International Spy Museum
5. FBI
6. National Archives
7. White House
8. Post Pub
9. Watergate Complex
10. Map of the Political Stars
11. Pentagon

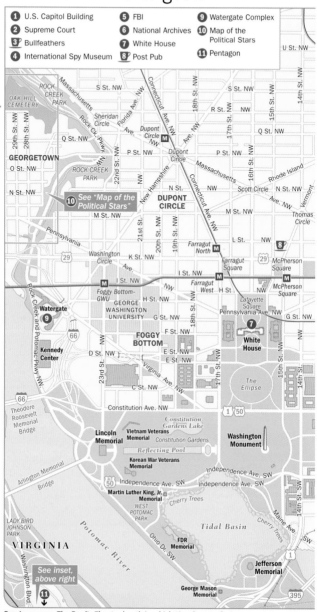

Previous page: The Ford's Theatre booth in which Lincoln was shot.

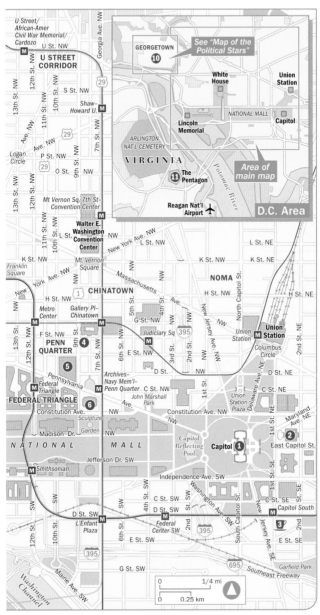

U Street/
African-Amer
Civil War Memorial/
Cardozo

U St. NW

**U STREET
CORRIDOR**

Georgia Ave. NW

(29)

S St. NW

Shaw-
Howard U.

*See "Map of the
Political Stars"*

GEORGETOWN
(10)

White
House

Union
Station

13th St. NW

12th St. NW

11th St. NW

10th St. NW

7th St. NW

9th St. NW

Ave. NW

(29)

P St. NW

Logan
Circle

(29)

O St. NW

NATIONAL MALL

Capitol

Lincoln
Memorial

ARLINGTON
NAT'L CEMETERY

VIRGINIA

Potomac River

13th St. NW

12th St. NW

9th St. NW

Mt Vernon Sq/
Convention Center

Walter E.
Washington
Convention
Center

**Area of
main map**

(11) **The
Pentagon**

**Reagan Nat'l
Airport** ✈

D.C. Area

Franklin
Square

K St. NW

NW

L St.

L St. NW

New York Ave. NW

K St. NW

L St. NW

K St. NE

L St. NE

New

York Ave. NW

Mt. Vernon
Square

11th St. NW

10th St. NW

Massachusetts

H St. NW

New Jersey Ave. NW

North Capitol St.

H St. NW

H St. NE

(1)

CHINATOWN

H St. NW

NW

5th St. NW

4th St.

Ave.

NOMA

13th St.

Metro
Center

Gallery Pl-
Chinatown

F St. NW

G St. NW

Judiciary Sq

(395)

Union
Station

**Union
Station**

2nd St. NE

**PENN
QUARTER**
(4)

9th St. NW

7th St. NW

6th St.

E St.

Union
Station

Columbus
Circle

12th St. NW

(5)

Pennsylvania

Archives-
Navy Mem'l-
Penn Quarter

C St. NW

D St.

1st St.

Union
Station
Plaza

Delaware Ave. NE

D St. NE

C St. NE

FEDERAL TRIANGLE
(6)

Federal
Triangle

John Marshall
Park

1st St.

Constitution Ave.

NW

Constitution Ave. NW

Maryland
Ave. NE

Constitution Ave.

NW

Sculpture

Madison Dr.

Garden

*Capitol
Reflecting
Pool*

Capitol (1)

1st St. SE

(2)
East Capitol St.

NATIONAL

MALL

Jefferson Dr. SW

Independence Ave. SW

Washington Ave. SW

Smithsonian

C St. SW

C St. SE

1st St. SE

12th St. SW

10th St. SW

SW

SW

D St. SW

4th St. SW

D St. SW

**Federal
Center SW**

6th St. SW

E St. SW

2nd

(395)

South Capitol St.

New

Jersey Ave. SE

E St. SE

Capitol South M
(3)

2nd

L'Enfant
Plaza

(395)

G St. SW

Maine Ave. SW

(695)

Southeast Freeway

Garfield Park

*Washington
Channel*

| 0 | 1/4 mi |

| 0 | 0.25 km |

Oh, the intrigue . . . the drama . . . the repressed yawns from members of Congress as they fight to stay awake during marathon legislative sessions on Capitol Hill. Exciting or not, Washington is pure politics, 24/7. If you live here, there's no escape from the maneuverings of our elected officials, and the (sometimes biting, sometimes toothless) press corps that hounds them. If you're visiting, spend a few days catching a glimpse of the capital's complex, consequential, and at times truly captivating political scene, from past to present, with this tour. START: **Metro to Capitol South or Union Station**

① ★★★ **U.S. Capitol Building.** Viewed from the wide avenues that radiate toward and away from it, the Capitol is almost palatial in its grandeur, crowning the highest point between the Potomac and Anacostia rivers. Connected to the White House by a grand diagonal avenue (Pennsylvania Ave.), the Capitol was part of architect Pierre L'Enfant's plan to represent the separation of powers in the capital grid and architecture when he laid out the city in 1791. The Capitol complex includes the Capitol, the House and Senate Office Buildings, the U.S. Botanic Garden, the Capitol Grounds, the Library of Congress buildings, and the Supreme Court Building. Among the Capitol's most impressive features are the cast-iron dome, the rotunda, the old Senate and Supreme Court chambers, the Brumidi Corridors, and the National Statuary Hall. When you tour the building, you'll see interior embellishments that include richly patterned and colored floor tiles, the vaulted and ornately decorated corridors on the first floor of the Senate wing, and the fluted white marble pillars lining the Hall of Columns, plus hundreds of paintings, sculptures, and other artworks, including the 4,664-square-foot (433 sq. m) fresco *The Apotheosis of Washington.* In late 2008, the experience of visiting the Capitol changed monumentally with the opening of the Capitol Visitor Center. This half billion-dollar complex, located beneath the Capitol itself, has an exhibition hall featuring the Statue of Freedom, amendments to the Constitution, and an 11-foot-tall (3.4m) model of the Capitol Dome. Hands-on exhibits include virtual tours of the building and touchable reproductions of famous Capitol artworks. Remember—food, beverages, large bags, and pointed objects are prohibited on these tours. ⏱ *2 hr. East end of the Mall (entrance on E. Capitol and 1st sts. NW).* ☎ *202/226-8000.*

Politicos on the famous Capitol steps.

The Old Supreme Court Chamber in the Capitol Building.

www.aoc.gov, www.house.gov, www.visitthecapitol.gov, or www. senate.gov. Mon–Sat, 1st tour at 8:50am and last at 3:20pm. Closed Jan 1, Thanksgiving, and Dec 25. Metro: Capitol South or Union Station.

❷ ★★ **Supreme Court.** Whether they're debating about constitutionality, voting over dimpled chads, or walking a social tightrope over controversial federal laws, the nation's nine Supreme Court justices, who are appointed for life terms, cast their votes here. Where the buck stops when it comes to determining the liberties of Americans, the chamber of the highest court in the land has been restored to its mid-19th-century appearance. It's worth visiting, if only to see for yourself how justice prevails—or sometimes doesn't.

The Court convenes on the first Monday in October and stays in session until it has heard all of its cases and handed down its decisions. It hears oral arguments the Monday, Tuesday, and Wednesday of the first 2 weeks of each month. Visitors can listen to the arguments on short tours, or they can watch the entire day's proceedings. **Note:** If you are a legal eagle or Court TV fanatic bent on spending the whole day here, arrive by 8:30am to get in line early; seating is first-come, first-served. ⏰ *2 hr. 1st and E. Capitol sts. NE.* ☎ *202/479-3211. www.supremecourtus.gov. Free admission. Mon–Fri 9am–4:30pm, except federal holidays. Lines can be long; be prepared to wait for up to 1 hr. Metro: Capitol South or Union Station.*

Legislative Sessions Live

If you wish to visit the House and/or Senate galleries while they are in session, you'll need a pass from your congressional representative, or from your sergeant-at-arms if you live in the District (and suffer "taxation without representation"). The House gallery is open weekdays from 9am to 4:15pm when the House is not in session; the Senate gallery is open during scheduled recesses of 1 week or more, weekdays from 9am to 4:15pm. Entry to both galleries is through the Capitol Visitor Center on the upper level. Call ☎ **202/ 226-8000** or go to www.visitthecapitol.gov.

Bullfeathers, steps from the Capitol Building and named for the euphemism Teddy Roosevelt used to avoid swearing while in office, is the place for hungry Hill staffers and politicos to enjoy burgers and bar food, among other American classics. *410 1st St. SE. ☎ 202/484-0228. www. bullfeathersdc.com. $–$$. Metro: Capitol South.*

④ ★★ **International Spy Museum.** James Bond, eat your heart out. This place makes your "high-tech" gadgetry seem, well, quaint. Come tour the real deal, the first American museum dedicated to the art of espionage. Learn about Soviet double agents, attend any of a revolving assortment of expert lectures, view the spy treasures from Hollywood films, play spy games, and do other super cool, super sneaky stuff. ⏱ *2 hr. 800 F St. NW. ☎ 202/ EYE-SPYU [393-7798]. www. spymuseum.org. Admission $20 adults, $15 seniors, $14 kids 7–11, free for kids 6 and under. Hours change monthly; see website for details. Metro: Gallery Place/Chinatown.*

A shoe camera at the International Spy Museum.

⑤ **FBI.** The highest level of American law enforcement, the Federal Bureau of Investigation is headquartered on Pennsylvania Avenue, between 9th and 10th streets, in the J. Edgar Hoover Building. While it once offered public tours, these have been suspended indefinitely. But that shouldn't stop you from buying an FBI sweatshirt from a street vendor, and telling the kids back home you toured it anyway. ⏱ *20 min. 935 Pennsylvania Ave. NW. ☎ (202) 324-3447. www.fbi.gov. Metro: Federal Triangle or Archives.*

⑥ **National Archives.** How else can you experience the founding of our nation's government than by seeing the documents that started it all? The Constitution, the Declaration of Independence, and the Bill of Rights are here, along with countless other materials such as Abraham Lincoln's telegrams to his generals and audio recordings from the Oval Office. Advanced reservations are highly recommended, as the wait to get in can be as long as an hour at the height of tourist season (mid-Mar through Labor Day). Guided tours are offered at 9:45am Monday to

The Guardian of Law, *outside the U.S. Supreme Court.*

The International Spy Museum.

Friday, or you can book a Timed Visit Entry, 10am to 90 minutes before closing. ⏱ *1½ hr. Constitution Ave. NW (btw. 7th & 9th sts.). 877/444-6777. Free admission. 10am–7pm (Mar 15 to Labor Day); 10am–5:30pm (Day after Labor Day to Mar 14), Closed Thanksgiving and Dec 25.*

⑦ ★★★ White House.

President John Adams and his wife, Abigail, were the first tenants, back in 1800, and every subsequent U.S. president and his wife have lived here since. President Barack Obama and his wife, Michelle, planted an organic garden on its lawn and even built a play set for daughters Malia and Sasha on the south grounds. But the White House has seen its share of drama over the years: It endured a fire set by invading British troops in 1812; survived another blaze in 1929 during Herbert Hoover's presidency; lived down President Clinton's Oval Office shenanigans in the late 1990s; and even served as a backdrop for the Aaron Sorkin series, *The West Wing,* taking drama to an Emmy-winning level. If you wish to tour its legendary rooms—from the elegant reception area of the Blue Room to the Yellow Oval Room, where state guests are entertained before or

The official seal of the Federal Bureau of Investigation.

after official luncheons—you must do so in a group of 10 or more. You also need to make an official request and submit it through your representative in Congress. These self-guided tours are scheduled on a first-come, first-served basis and need to be made at least 1 month in advance of your visit. To enhance your experience, stop by the White House Visitor Center to view exhibitions on the architecture, furnishings, events, and social history of America's First Address. ⏱ *1 hr.; come early for an unobstructed view through the iron fence and skip any elbowing to get close. 1600 Pennsylvania Ave. NW. ☎ 202/456-7041 (24-hr. information hotline). www.whitehouse.gov. Free admission. Tour times vary; visitor center: daily 7:30am–4pm. Closed on federal holidays. Metro: Federal Triangle and McPherson Sq.*

The *Washington Post*—immortalized by Bob Woodward and Carl Bernstein's dogged reporting on the Watergate scandal—at once exposes and greases the political machinery of the capital. Stop by the ⑧ ★★ **Post Pub,** where legions

A protest in front of the White House.

of ink-stained scribes come to slam a beer after a hard day fact-checking the latest innuendo, accusation, or blatant lie issued by one of the U.S.'s fearless leaders. See p 151.

⑨ Watergate Complex.

Remember when the Watergate Hotel was synonymous only with Nixon, botched burglaries, and Woodward and Bernstein? Now, when you walk by this Washington legend, you can't help but think of another salacious scandal that found its orbit here: The adjacent Watergate condo complex is where Monica Lewinsky hid for 9 months from a stalking press corps after news broke of her affair with President Bill Clinton. She left the residence in October 1998, leaving a

note of apology to her neighbors. ⏱ 10 min. Condo complex: 700 New Hampshire Ave. NW. Metro: Foggy Bottom.

⑩ Map of the Political Stars.

If you've ever cruised around Beverly Hills, California, you've seen the signs selling "Star Maps" that pinpoint the gated entrances to your favorite celebrities' private dwellings. In a city that has famously been described as "Hollywood for Ugly People," a map of the political stars is appropriate. Politicos and the journalists who cover them set up house all around the District, but Georgetown is like the North Star when it comes to finding government types past and present. This tour focuses on this enclave for the rich and powerful—the Beverly Hills of the nation's capital. ⏱ 2 hr.

The infamous Watergate Complex.

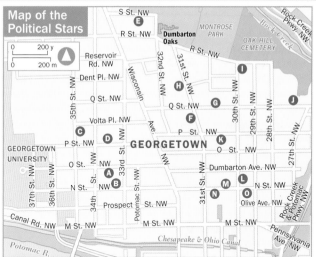

Map of the Political Stars

A John Kerry residence. A residence of the senator and former presidential candidate (3322 O St. NW).
B John and Jackie Kennedy house. Their home before moving into the White House (3307 N St. NW).
C Alexander Graham Bell residence. Home of the inventor of the telephone—not a political figure per se, but one whose contributions were to have a huge impact on the future of the nation (1527 35th St. NW).
D John Edwards residence. The former senator and his family live here. It's also the former home of CIA head Frank Wisner. Legend has it that many CIA agents lived along Q Street during the Agency's founding years (3327 P St. NW). **E John Warner and Elizabeth Taylor home**—once upon a time (3240 S St. NW).
F John F. Kennedy residence. He lived here after first being elected to Congress from Massachusetts' 11th District (1528 31st St. NW).
G Bob Woodward residence. Home of the Watergate reporter (3027 Q St. NW). **H Tudor Place.** Once home to six generations of Martha Washington's descendants, it's

now a museum (1644 31st St. NW).
I Katharine Graham residence. Former home of the woman who guided the *Washington Post* for decades (2920 R St. NW). **J Dumbarton House.** Originally belonged to Joseph Nourse, register of the Treasury for six presidents (2715 Q St. NW). **K Henry Kissinger residence.** Home of the superdiplomat (3026 P St. NW).
L Miss Lydia English's Georgetown Female Seminary. Visited by Martin Van Buren, James Buchanan, and Daniel Webster. Later served as a Union Army hospital (1311 30th St. NW). **M Jackie Kennedy residence.** She lived here briefly following JFK's assassination (3017 N St. NW). **N Pamela and W. Averell Harriman residence.** Home of the politician, diplomat, and businessman W. Averell Harriman and his third wife, the socialite and political activist Pamela Churchill Harriman (3038 N St. NW). **O Foxhall House.** Residence of Henry Foxhall, whose foundry provided guns for the War of 1812 (2908 N St. NW).

President Richard Nixon, who made the Watergate infamous.

⓫ ★★★ **Pentagon.** The headquarters for the Department of Defense is one of the world's largest office buildings, holding approximately 23,000 government workers, both military and civilian. Perhaps only the White House figures as much into the collective consciousness as this structure. Popularized in Hollywood movies, it was scarred on the tragic day of September 11, 2001, when a hijacked airliner ripped into its west side, killing 125 workers and 59 passengers. The building smoldered for days. But, incredibly, the gash in its wall was repaired within 6 months and new offices were constructed by the 1-year anniversary of the attack. In dedication to the lives lost in the attack, the Pentagon 9/11 Memorial was constructed and unveiled on September 11, 2008. It consists of 184 benches—one for each victim— that range in height to represent the youngest and oldest victims of the attack. It's free and open to the public every day. Visitors who want to tour the building and pay their respects will need to reserve a group tour at least 2 weeks (and a maximum of 3 months) in advance. ⏲ *2 hr. including commute. Off I-395.* ☎ *703/697-1776. http://pentagon. afis.osd.mil. To submit your tour request, go to the website and click "Tours." Free admission. Metro: Pentagon.*

The 9/11 Memorial at the Pentagon.

The Hay-Adams Hotel's Off the Record Bar, considered to be one of the world's best hotel bars.

Where Politicos Drink & Dine

Art and Soul ★★ (415 New Jersey Ave. NW; ☎ 202/393-7777), in the Liaison Hotel on Capitol Hill, is a favorite among the power-tie/ pumps-and-pearls-set for breakfast, lunch, and dinner. Also on the Hill, the dive bars Tune Inn (332 Pennsylvania Ave. SE; ☎ 202/543-2725) and Pour House (319 Pennsylvania Ave. SE; ☎ 202/546-0779), with their quirky decors, are the perfect spots to eavesdrop on the scuttlebutt of young Hill staffers, who flock here after work. In Penn Quarter, the Capital Grille (601 Pennsylvania Ave. NW; ☎ 202/737-6200) is ground zero for cigars, Scotch, steaks, suspenders, and high-level lobbying. Catch prominent members of Congress wheeling and dealing at Charlie Palmer Steak (101 Constitution Ave. NW; ☎ 202/547-8100), a mainstay for tasty lunchtime steaks and crab cakes. Steps from the White House, in the Hay-Adams Hotel, Off the Record Bar (800 16th St. NW; ☎ 202/638-6600) serves stiff drinks to power mongers. And John Boswell—four-time *Washingtonian* magazine "Best Bartender" winner—pretends not to overhear state secrets. The very preppy Smith Point (1338 Wisconsin Ave. NW; ☎ 202/333-9003) is a hot spot for SUV-driving Young Republicans; it's where to head for Nantucket-style entrees—and the latest looks in Lacoste wear.

D.C. for **Architecture Lovers**

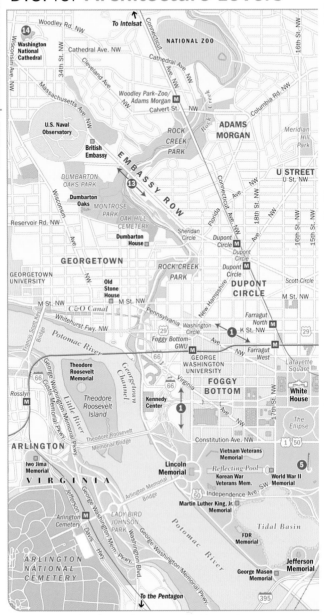

- **14** Washington National Cathedral
- Woodley Rd. NW
- To Intelsat
- Cathedral Ave. NW
- NATIONAL ZOO
- 34th St. NW
- Cleveland Ave.
- Cathedral Ave. NW
- Wisconsin Ave. NW
- Woodley Park-Zoo/ Adams Morgan M
- Calvert St. NW
- Columbia Rd. NW
- 16th St. NW
- Massachusetts Ave. NW
- U.S. Naval Observatory
- ADAMS MORGAN
- ROCK CREEK PARK
- Rock Creek
- Meridian Hill Park
- British Embassy
- EMBASSY ROW
- **13**
- DUMBARTON OAKS PARK
- Dumbarton Oaks
- MONTROSE PARK
- OAK HILL CEMETERY
- Florida Ave. NW
- U STREET
- U St. NW
- 18th St. NW
- 16th St. NW
- 15th St. NW
- Connecticut Ave. NW
- Reservoir Rd. NW
- Wisconsin Ave. NW
- Dumbarton House
- Sheridan Circle
- Dupont Circle M
- GEORGETOWN
- ROCK CREEK PARK
- Dupont Circle
- Dupont Circle M
- DUPONT CIRCLE
- New Hampshire Ave.
- Scott Circle
- GEORGETOWN UNIVERSITY
- Old Stone House
- M St. NW
- M St. NW
- M St. NW
- C&O Canal
- Whitehurst Fwy. NW
- Pennsylvania Ave.
- Washington Circle
- 29
- Farragut North M
- K St. NW
- 29
- Francis Scott Key Bridge
- Potomac River
- Georgetown Channel
- Foggy Bottom-GWU M
- Virginia Ave.
- Farragut West M
- Lafayette Square
- Rosslyn
- Theodore Roosevelt Memorial
- **1**
- GEORGE WASHINGTON UNIVERSITY
- FOGGY BOTTOM
- 17th St. NW
- White House
- 66
- George Washington Memorial Pkwy.
- Custis Memorial Pkwy.
- Theodore Roosevelt Island
- 66
- Kennedy Center
- **1**
- The Ellipse
- 1 50
- ARLINGTON
- Iwo Jima Memorial
- Little River
- Theodore Roosevelt Memorial Bridge
- Constitution Ave. NW
- VIRGINIA
- Arlington Memorial Bridge
- Lincoln Memorial
- Vietnam Veterans Memorial
- Reflecting Pool
- Korean War Veterans Mem.
- World War II Memorial
- **5**
- Arlington M Cemetery
- George Washington Memorial Pkwy.
- LADY BIRD JOHNSON PARK
- Independence Ave. SW
- Martin Luther King, Jr. Memorial
- Tidal Basin
- ARLINGTON NATIONAL CEMETERY
- Jefferson Davis Hwy.
- Washington Blvd.
- Potomac River
- FDR Memorial
- George Washington Memorial Pkwy.
- George Mason Memorial
- Jefferson Memorial
- To the Pentagon
- 395

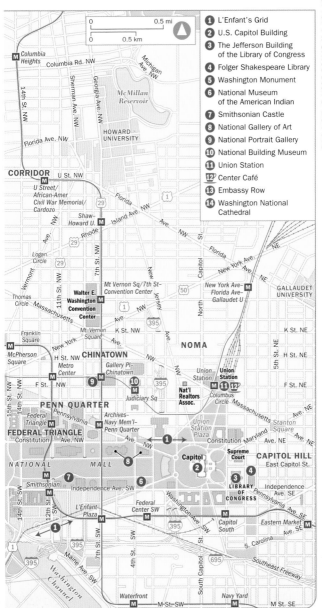

1. L'Enfant's Grid
2. U.S. Capitol Building
3. The Jefferson Building of the Library of Congress
4. Folger Shakespeare Library
5. Washington Monument
6. National Museum of the American Indian
7. Smithsonian Castle
8. National Gallery of Art
9. National Portrait Gallery
10. National Building Museum
11. Union Station
12. Center Café
13. Embassy Row
14. Washington National Cathedral

talian journalist Beppe Severgnini wrote *Ciao, America: An Italian Discovers the U.S.*, which details his experience living in a historic Georgetown row house. He echoes the sentiments I've heard among many expat Europeans in Washington: that despite the stark foreignness of America—the fast-food, techno-obsessed, impatient, kid-worshiping culture of this country—at least, in D.C., there is the architecture. The buildings here evoke the grand structures of Paris and the historically wrought designs of London, with the neoclassical embellishments of both—Roman-style pillars, carved flourishes, and weathered stone lions perched on guard before public entrances.

START: **Metro to Capitol South or Union Station**

❶ L'Enfant's Grid. Designed in 1791 by French engineer Pierre L'Enfant, the District's street plan—a conventional city grid overlaid with grand, diagonal avenues—mimics the layout of many great European cities. Designed to represent the separation of powers and the balance between state and federal government, the grid links the Capitol and the White House via the grand Pennsylvania Avenue. Diagonal avenues are named for the states. The 2½-mile-long (4km), 400-foot-wide (122m) esplanade known as the National Mall links the White House with the Washington Monument.

Washington fired L'Enfant, whose grand scheme prevailed but took more than a century to build, with major snafus along the way (the British torched the White

House, the Capitol Building, and the Library of Congress in 1814). But D.C.'s centennial in 1900 brought renewed interest in and commitment to L'Enfant's vision, which served as a blueprint for the redesign of the city by the likes of Frederick Law Olmstead, Daniel Burnham, and Charles McKim. ⏱ *20 min. To see L'Enfant's original drawings and other historical documents, visit the Library of Congress, p 57.*

❷ ★★★ U.S. Capitol Building. Washington's architecture is about neoclassical harmony and a fierce reverence for the era that birthed the nation's capital, and no building better exemplifies these values than the Capitol itself. Amateur architect George Washington praised the original plans for the building, drafted by Dr. William Thornton, for

The Washington Monument and the Capitol Building from across the Potomac.

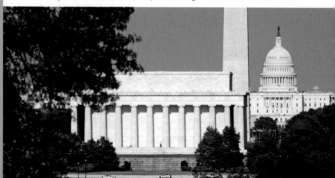

The I. M. Pei wing of the National Gallery.

their "grandeur, simplicity, and convenience." Construction, however, was anything but simple. When Congress first met here in November 1800, it was still under construction. Begun in 1793, the project would take 34 years and six architects to complete. Even then, it was too small for its occupants, and a second round of construction lasted through 1851. Lincoln insisted that the expansion continue during the Civil War. The neoclassical structure now covers 4 acres (1.6 hectares) and is 288 feet (88m) tall, including the Statue of Freedom. 🕐 *2 hr. See p 28.*

❸ ★ **Jefferson Building of the Library of Congress.** A much smaller version of the Library of Congress originally sat inside the new Capitol, but the British destroyed it upon sacking the city during the War of 1812. In its place, Thomas Jefferson offered his personal library. In 1886, Congress finally authorized construction of a larger Italian Renaissance–style library, designed by local architects John L. Smithmeyer and Paul J. Pelz.

Coming years saw the addition of an equally impressive interior with works by more than 50 American artists, commissioned by architect Edward Pearce Casey. In the Main Reading Room, crane your neck to see the dome 160 feet (49m) above; the cupola is a female figure painted by artist Edwin Blashfield, representing "Human Understanding." 🕐 *1 hr. 10 1st St. SE.* ☎ *202/707-8000.*

Folger Shakespeare Library.

www.loc.gov. Free admission. Obtain same-day free tickets to tour the library inside the west entrance on 1st St. Mon–Sat 8:30am–4:30pm. Closed federal holidays. Metro: Capitol South.

❹ Folger Shakespeare Library.

The marble exterior of this neoclassical building blends harmoniously with the nearby Library of Congress and Supreme Court, but the interior is pure Tudor England, complete with oak paneling and plaster ceilings. The building was designed by Paul Philippe Cret, but the Shakespeare bas-reliefs on the exterior were designed by John Gregory. Masks of Comedy and Tragedy hang above the doors. 🕐 *30 min. 201 E. Capitol St. SE.* ☎ *202/544-7077. www.folger.edu. Free admission. Mon–Sat 10am–5pm: Sun noon– 5pm; free walk-in tours daily at 11am and 1pm on Sun. Closed federal holidays. Metro: Capitol South or Union Station.*

❺ Washington Monument.

The idea for a national monument to George Washington began as early as 1783, but construction on this Egyptian-style obelisk in the center of the National Mall didn't begin until 1848. Designed by famed architect Robert Mills, work on the monument was stopped in 1854 due to lack of funds. To this day, you can see the

The exterior of the National Museum of the American Indian.

difference in color between the marble at the bottom and that at the top. It was the tallest building in the world until the Eiffel Tower's completion in 1889, and it's still the tallest in D.C. 🕐 *45 min. See p 53.*

❻ ★★ National Museum of the American Indian. A team of Native architects and consultants

Curbing Vertical Sprawl

In 1899, Congress passed the Heights of Building Act, which stipulated that no private structure within the District could rise higher than the Capitol Building or other important government edifice—meaning the city would never boast the skyscrapers of other towns. (A later act amended this height restriction to 130 ft./40m, and made exceptions for spires, towers, and domes.) This merely challenged contemporary architects to soar to new "heights"; modern design here is concise but nonetheless stunning.

designed this pueblo-like museum, constructed of Kasota stone, on the National Mall. With its curved facade and angled placement, the building aligns with Native American beliefs in the cardinal points. The grounds include cascading water, as well as wetlands of wild rice, marsh marigolds, corn, native tree species, and indigenous plants to honor local Native people. ⏱ *1½ hr. 4th St. & Independence Ave. SW.* ☎ *202/633-1000. Free admission. Daily 10am–5:30pm, except Dec 25. www.nmai.si.edu. Metro: L'Enfant Plaza.*

⑦ Smithsonian Castle. From museums to monuments, marble is de rigueur for buildings along the National Mall. So no wonder this Gothic Castle, placed squarely in the middle of the lot, sticks out. Architect James Renwick, Jr., of St. Patrick's Cathedral in New York, designed the original Smithsonian Institution Building in 1855, and constructed it of red sandstone from nearby Seneca Creek, MD. The classic structure is now home base for the Smithsonian Information Center and its gallery. ⏱ *30 min. 1000 Jefferson Dr. SW.* ☎ *202/633-1000. www.si.edu. Free*

admission. Daily, 8:30am–5:30pm. Metro: Smithsonian.

⑧ National Gallery of Art. The museum's triangular-shaped East Building—with its acute-angled stone corners, designed in 1978 by I. M. Pei—may look worlds apart from the neoclassical West Building across the plaza, but its marble was cut from the same quarry in Tennessee. The West Building, which resembles the nearby Museum of Natural History, was designed by John Russell Pope in 1941. ⏱ *1 hr. See p 12.*

⑨ ★★★ National Portrait Gallery. Designed by a number of prominent architects, including Robert Mills (designer of the Washington Monument), this museum was the third public building constructed in the city, after the Capitol and the White House. During the Civil War, it served as the site of Lincoln's second inaugural ball as well as a hospital for soldiers. Although it's a notable example of Greek Revival architecture, it was almost demolished in the 1950s before the Smithsonian Institution took over its control. It closed in 2001 for a

The National Gallery's East Building Atrium.

5-year renovation project that added more exhibition space, an auditorium, and an enclosed courtyard featuring a dramatic glass-and-steel roof. ⏱ *1 hr. 8th and F sts. NW (in the U.S. Patent Office Building).* ☎ *202/638-8300. www.npg.si.edu. Free admission. Call for hours. Metro: Gallery Place/Chinatown.*

⑩ National Building Museum.

With regular exhibitions devoted to art and architecture, this palatial brick museum took roughly 5 years to build and was modeled after Italy's monumental Palazzo Farnese that Michelangelo commissioned in 1589. The massive Great Hall of the building holds colossal Corinthian columns—among the tallest in the world—and extends 116 x 316 feet (35 x 96m). A fountain bisects the hall, stretching 28 feet (8.5m) across. Strategically placed windows, vents, and archways are part of a unique ventilation system that whisks a continuous flow of fresh air through the building. ⏱ *1 hr. 401 F St. NW.* ☎ *202/272-2448. www. nbm.org. $8 adults; $5 youth, students, and seniors. Mon–Sat 10am–5pm; Sun 11am–5pm. Metro: Judiciary Square.*

Embassy Row.

⑪ Union Station.

When master architect Daniel Burnham designed this Beaux Arts–style building, he was determined to make it a grand gateway for a magnificent city, complete with 96-foot (29m) ceilings inlaid with 70 pounds (32kg) of 22-karat gold leaf. Upon its completion in 1908, Union Station was the largest train station in the world; if laid on its side, the Washington Monument would fit into its concourse. Its original area, along with the terminal zone, totaled 200 acres (81 hectares) and included 75 miles (121km) of track. It was also enormously expensive, costing roughly $125 million to build. ⏱ *45 min. 2 Massachusetts Ave. NE.* ☎ *202/289-1908. www.unionstationdc.com. Free admission. Daily 24 hr. Metro: Union Station.*

Linger over the view of Union Station's opulent atrium while enjoying a quick bite of American fare at the ⑫ **Center Café.** *Union Station, 2 Massachusetts Ave. NW;* ☎ *202/ 682-3042; arkrestaurants.com. $. Metro: Union Station.*

⑬ ★★ Embassy Row.

This stretch of Massachusetts Avenue from Dupont Circle to the National Cathedral is where the majority of foreign embassies and ambassadors reside. Sir Edwin Lutyens—an architect of the late 19th and early 20th centuries, renowned for his English country houses and remodeled castles—designed the British Embassy in 1928. This prominent Embassy Row structure is notable for its tall chimneys and high roofs, suggestive of the Queen Anne period. From this traditional design to the contemporary glass wall that juts over Rock Creek Park at the Finnish embassy, there's no shortage of architectural inspiration along this tour. ⏱ *2 hr. Begin:*

Massachusetts Ave. NW at Dupont Circle and head North. Metro: Dupont Circle.

⓮ ★★★ **Washington National Cathedral.** More than 200 stained-glass windows adorn this classic Gothic-style cathedral, the second largest in the United States and sixth largest in the world; one of them has a rock from the moon embedded in its center. The building, made largely of gray Indiana limestone and completed in 1990 after 2 centuries of planning and more than 80 years of work, contains a number of magnificent woodcarvings, metal work, and other artworks. Frederick Bodley, an Anglican Church architect, originally oversaw the project (with supervision by architect Henry Vaughan), but Philip Hubert Frohman took over after World War I. The top of the cathedral tower is the highest point in the city. ⏲ *1 hr. See p 21.*

The magnificent interior of the Washington National Cathedral.

Strong Foundations

While not open for public tours, a handful of architectural sites around D.C. are known for their cutting-edge design. Graham Gund Architects of Cambridge, Massachusetts, designed the 12-story **National Realtors Association** headquarters (500 New Jersey Ave. NW; ☎ **800/874-6500;** free tours by appointment only; Metro: Judiciary Sq.) to be environmentally sustainable, with recycled materials, permeability to natural light to reduce energy costs, and a carbon dioxide monitoring system to introduce more fresh air into highly populated areas. Built in 1987, the **Intelsat** building (3400 International Dr. NW; ☎ **202/944-6800;** www.intelsat.com; free tours by appointment only; Metro: Van Ness/UDC) has a unique facade, designed by John Andrews International, that provides natural lighting to the "office pods" inside and conserves energy.

Washington **for Kids**

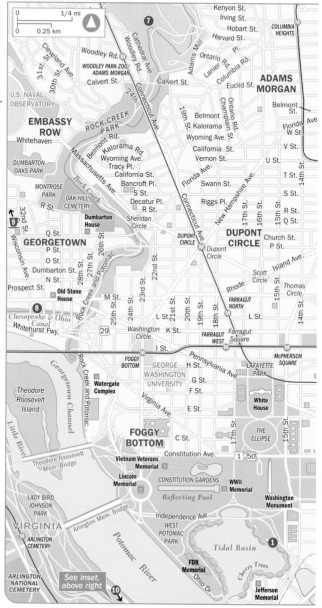

Kenyon St.
Irving St.
Columbia Rd.
Harvard St.
Girard St.
Fairmont St.
Euclid St.

HOWARD UNIVERSITY

13th St. 12th St. 11th St. 10th St. 9th St. 8th St.
Barry Pl.

U STREET CORRIDOR

U STREET-CARDOZO

SHAW-HOWARD UNIVERSITY

Rhode Island Ave.

7th St. 6th St. 5th St. 4th St. 3rd St.

Florida Ave.

North Capitol St.

BRENTWOOD PARK

Logan Circle

(29) (1)

N St.

M St.

New York Ave.

13th St. 12th St. 11th St. 10th St. 9th St. 8th St.

DOWNTOWN

New York Ave.

(1)

CHINATOWN

Mt. Vernon Square

MT. VERNON SQ./ CONVENTION CTR.
(1)

(50)

Massachusetts Ave.

New Jersey Ave.

K St.
I St.
H St.
G St.

1st St.

UNION STATION

Union Station

GALLERY PLACE-CHINATOWN

3rd St. 2nd St. 1st St.

F St.
E St.

METRO CENTER

❺ ❻

PENN QUARTER

❷

JUDICIARY SQUARE

D St.

Louisiana Ave.

Delaware Ave.

Stanton Square

FEDERAL TRIANGLE

Pennsylvania Ave.

ARCHIVES-NAVY MEMORIAL

C St.

Maryland

A St.
East Capitol St.
A St.

❸

Constitution Ave.

CAPITOL HILL

NATIONAL MALL

Madison Dr.

U.S. Capitol

SMITHSONIAN

❹ Jefferson Dr.

Independence Ave.

New Jersey Ave.

Seward Square

North Carolina Ave.

L'ENFANT PLAZA

FEDERAL CENTER SW

Washington Ave.

CAPITOL SOUTH

Pennsylvania Ave.

EASTERN MARKET

Washington Channel

South Capitol St.

(395)

D.C. Area

Area of main map

ROCK CREEK PARK

White House

Union Station

NATIONAL MALL

Lincoln Memorial

U.S. Capitol

ARLINGTON NATIONAL CEMETERY

Potomac River

The Pentagon

VIRGINIA

❿

Reagan Nat'l Airport

❶ Tidal Basin
❷ National Building Museum
❸ National Museum of Natural History
❹ National Air and Space Museum
❺ International Spy Museum
❻ Spy City Café
❼ National Zoological Park
❽ C&O Canal Towpath
❾ 2 Amys
❿ Gravelly Point

Here's a bold statement: Disney World included, there is no better place to take the kids on vacation than Washington, D.C. The District is overflowing with the stuff of a memorable field trip—pandas, dinosaur bones, spy gadgets, rocket ships, insect gardens, historical monuments—and much of it is free. There's even a park, adjacent to Ronald Reagan National Airport, that's so close to the runways, you feel as though planes are landing on top of you. Ask any kid—nothing is cooler than this. Allow at least 2 days to complete this tour, or pick and choose the stops you wish to visit, depending on your kids' attention span and level of interest. START: **Metro to Smithsonian**

❶ ★★★ Paddle boats on the Tidal Basin. The Jefferson Memorial overlooks the serene waters of the Tidal Basin, dotted with paddle boats on sunny days. Rent a boat and marry a history lesson with some exercise—and see the monuments and cherry blossoms from a beautiful and unique vantage point. ⏱ *1 hr. 1501 Maine Ave. SW (15th St.).* ☎ *202/479-2426. 2-passenger boat $12 per hr.; 4-passenger boat $19 per hr. Mar 15 to mid-Oct daily 10am–6pm. Metro: Smithsonian.*

❷ ★★ National Building Museum. If the weather is blistering or freezing and the kids need to blow off some steam, then head to this museum. The colossal Great Hall, which has hosted 15 presidential inaugural balls, is the perfect place to let them run indoors. Bring your own food and have a picnic inside, or head to the museum's Building Zone, ideal for visitors ages 2 to 6. Children can build towers and walls, drive bulldozers and play trucks, or work on any number of arts and crafts projects. ⏱ *1 hr. 401 F St. NW* ☎ *202/272-2448. www. nbm.org. $8 adults; $5 youth, students, and seniors. Mon–Fri 10am–5pm; Sun 11am–5pm. Metro: Judiciary Square or Gallery Place/ Chinatown.*

❸ ★★ National Museum of Natural History. Founded in 1846, this enormous repository for animal and plant specimens, many long extinct, includes the remains of 46 dinosaurs—guaranteed to wow even the most Nintendo-obsessed kids. Look for the stegosaurus in the Hall of Dinosaurs on the first floor. Kids love the huge African bush elephant that greets you at the Mall-facing entrance, the expansive Ocean Hall with its 274 living specimens, and the first-floor Discovery Room filled with creative hands-on exhibits "for children of all ages." The outdoor Butterfly Habitat Garden, on the 9th Street side of the building, is another crowd-pleaser: The 11,000-square-foot (1,022-sq.-m) area of winding trails and lush vegetation supports an estimated 26 species of butterflies. The garden cultivates interaction between these winged creatures and the plants

Tiger at the National Zoo.

The National Museum of Natural History.

and flowers that attract them, educating and delighting visitors. ⏱ *1 hr. 10th St. and Constitution Ave. NW* ☎ *202/633-1000. www.mnh.si.edu. Free admission. Daily 10am–5:30pm (Fri–Sat, and in summer, until 7:30pm). Closed Dec 25. Metro: Smithsonian or Federal Triangle.*

④ ★★★ National Air and Space Museum. Containing the largest historical collection of air- and spacecraft in the world, this is the place to explore rocket ships that have shot to the stars, see real Russian and American spacesuits, view the Wright Brothers' plane and World War II bombers, and even inspect the earliest passenger planes (kids can walk through the fuselage of one). The number of craft suspended from the sky-high ceiling inspires lots of upturned heads and dropped jaws. The Lockheed Martin IMAX Theater, with its awesome 3-D effects, will transport your little ones to Mars or the moon. ⏱ *2 hr. Independence Ave. between 4th and 7th sts.* ☎ *202/ 633-2214. www.nasm.si.edu. Free admission. Daily 10am–5:30pm (until 7:30pm in summer), except Dec 25. Metro: Smithsonian or L'Enfant Plaza (Smithsonian Museums/Maryland Ave. exit).*

⑤ ★★ International Spy Museum. Older kids who think the zoo is for babies will love this place, the sole public museum dedicated to espionage in the world. They'll learn about Soviet double agents, view the spy treasures from Hollywood films, play spy games, watch informative films, and take part in other super-sneaky stuff in a range of interactive exhibits. An executive director who spent 36 years with the CIA and an advisory board including two former CIA directors, two former CIA disguise chiefs, and a retired KGB general ensure that the stuff you see here is 100% authoritative. ⏱ *1 hr. Metro: Gallery Place/Chinatown. See p 30.*

See p 30.

A gorilla at the National Zoo.

The **Spy City Café** is the perfect lunch spot for Spy Museum visitors. Dig into salads, soups, sandwiches, or pizzas against a backdrop of photos of spy sites around Washington—the spying capital of the world. *9th and F sts.* ☎ *202/654-0995. www.spy museum.org/spy-city-cafe. $.*

⑦ ★★★ National Zoological Park. Established in 1889, the National Zoo is home to some 500 species, many of them rare and/or endangered. It also occupies 163 acres (66 hectares) of beautifully landscaped and wooded land, wonderful for strolling and enjoying the sunshine. Start your tour with the famous pandas. ⏲ *2 hr. See p 15.*

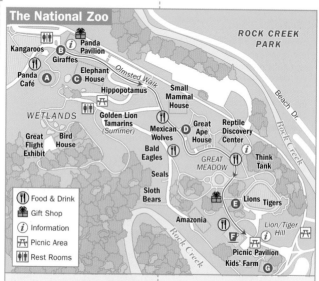

The National Zoo

Arguably the stars of the zoo, the giant pandas Mei Xiang and Tian Tian take center stage at the Ⓐ **FujiFilm Giant Panda Habitat.** Kids can't get enough of this animated, cuddly looking pair. Next, follow Ⓑ **Olmsted Walk** and you'll spot several natural habitats holding cheetahs, zebras, and kangaroos. An improved home for the Ⓒ **Asian elephants,** complete with a new elephant barn, two outdoor yards, and an Elephant Exercise Trek, is now in place. Off the main drag, you'll find natural wetlands and creatures ranging from bald eagles to seals. Farther south, at the Ⓓ **Great Ape House,** you can peer through glass walls at six gorillas

as they engage in startlingly human-like behaviors: grooming, wrestling, and even hugging one another. In the circular habitat of the Ⓔ **Great Cats,** south of the Great Ape House, lions and tigers sun themselves, their tails batting lazily as they gaze out at you. Stop for a bite at the cafeteria-style Ⓕ **Mane Grill,** which offers burgers, fries, chicken sandwiches, and other fast-food fare. Dine in or enjoy the nearby Picnic Pavilion. At the Ⓖ **Kids' Farm,** children 3 to 8 can meet and greet ducks, chickens, goats, cows, and miniature donkeys. Toddlers also love the nearby "pizza" playground.

8 C&O Canal Towpath. Have rambunctious little ones? Rent a bike at any nearby outfitter (see p 121 for specifics) and hit the C&O Canal Towpath. This tree-lined, picturesque gravelly trail follows a 19th-century canal that begins in Georgetown and heads west, ending 184 miles (296km) later in Cumberland, Maryland. It's a favorite of hikers, joggers, and bicyclists alike, and if you're looking to escape the bustle of the city or blow off steam after a day spent touring museums, you'll love it too. Two boat rental outfits near the start of the path rent kayaks and canoes. ⏱ *2 hr. No Metro access. See p 122.*

Mom and Dad need a drink, and the kids are ravenous. At **9** ★ **2 Amys**, they can dig into some authentic Neapolitan pizza while you savor lovely Italian red wine by the glass. *3715 Macomb St. NW.* ☎ *202/885-5700. www.2amyspizza.com. $$–$$$. No Metro access (a taxi is advised).*

10 Gravelly Point. If your kids are thrill-seekers, drive to this park that borders Reagan National Airport, minutes outside the District. (You'll need a car because no return taxis are available.) On any given day, you'll find teenagers, toddlers, and grandparents parked or picnicking on the grass, just feet from the airport runways. Gaze upward as jet after jet descends and flies directly overhead, so close you can read the markings on its underbelly—and then lands safely a short distance away. Not for the faint of heart! ⏱ *2 hr., including commute. Off the northbound George Washington Pkwy.* ☎ *703/289-2500.*

Child observing a stingray at the Kids' Farm.

Historic Washington

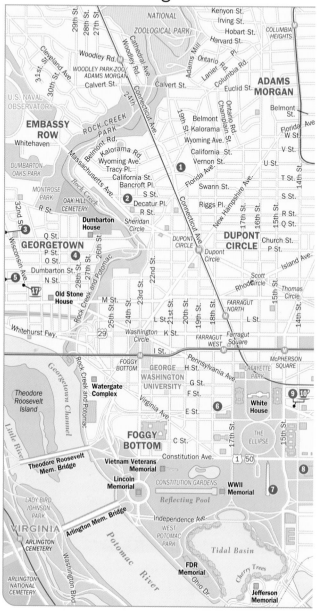

NATIONAL
ZOOLOGICAL PARK

Kenyon St.
Irving St.
Hobart St.
Harvard St.
COLUMBIA
HEIGHTS

29th St.
28th St.
27th St.

Woodley Rd.
Cathedral Ave.
Woodley Rd.

Adams Mill
Ontario Rd.
Lanier Rd.
Columbia Rd.

ADAMS
MORGAN

Cleveland Ave.
31st St.
30th St.

WOODLEY PARK-ZOO/
ADAMS MORGAN
Calvert St.
Calvert St.

24th St.

19th St.
Euclid St.

Belmont
St.

U.S. NAVAL
OBSERVATORY

EMBASSY
ROW

ROCK CREEK
PARK

Belmont Rd.
Kalorama Rd.
Wyoming Ave.
Tracy Pl.
California St.
Bancroft Pl.

Connecticut Ave.

Belmont
Kalorama
Wyoming Ave.
California St.
Vernon St.

Ontario Rd.
Champlain St.

Florida Ave.
W St.
V St.

Whitehaven

Massachusetts Ave.

Florida Ave.

U St.

14th St.

T St.
S St.

DUMBARTON
OAKS PARK

Rock Creek

Kalorama Rd.
Wyoming Ave.

Swann St.

17th St.
16th St.
15th St.

R St.
Q St.

MONTROSE
PARK

OAK HILL
CEMETERY

S St.
Decatur Pl.
R St.

Riggs Pl.

New Hampshire Ave.

Church St.
P St.

32nd St.

R St.

❶

Dumbarton
House

Sheridan
Circle

DUPONT
CIRCLE

3

Q St.

GEORGETOWN

❷

Dumbarton
House

Dupont
Circle

Island Ave.

Wisconsin Ave.

P St.
O St.

❹

26th St.

DUPONT
CIRCLE

Scott
Circle

Rhode

Thomas
Circle

❺

Dumbarton St.

28th St.

22nd St.

FARRAGUT
NORTH

14th St.

17

Old Stone
House

27th St.

N St.

23rd St.

21st St.
20th St.
19th St.
18th St.

L St.

Rock Creek and Potomac

25th St.
24th St.

M St.

L St.
K St.

FARRAGUT
WEST

Farragut
Square

Whitehurst Fwy.

29

Washington
Circle

I St.

FARRAGUT
WEST

McPHERSON
SQUARE

Pennsylvania Ave.

LAFAYETTE
PARK

Georgetown Channel

FOGGY
BOTTOM

GEORGE
WASHINGTON
UNIVERSITY

H St.
G St.
F St.

Theodore
Roosevelt
Island

Watergate
Complex

Virginia Ave.

E St.

❻

White
House

❾ ❿

Rock Creek and Potomac

Little River

FOGGY
BOTTOM

C St.

17th St.

THE
ELLIPSE

15th St.

Theodore Roosevelt
Mem. Bridge

Vietnam Veterans
Memorial

Constitution Ave.

❶ **50**

❽

LADY BIRD
JOHNSON
PARK

Lincoln
Memorial

CONSTITUTION GARDENS

Reflecting Pool

WEST
POTOMAC
PARK

WWII
Memorial

❼

VIRGINIA

ARLINGTON
CEMETERY

Arlington Mem. Bridge

Independence Ave.

Potomac River

Tidal Basin

Washington Blvd.

ARLINGTON
NATIONAL
CEMETERY

FDR
Memorial

Ohio Dr.

Cherry Trees

Jefferson
Memorial

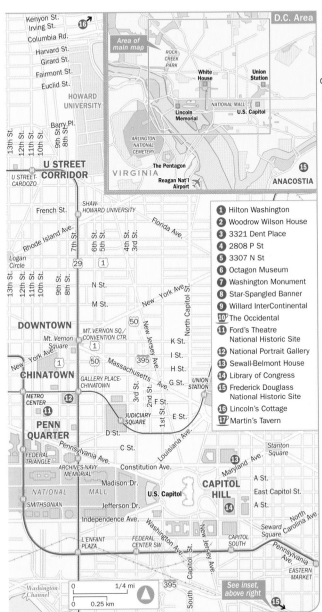

D.C. Area

Area of main map

ROCK CREEK PARK

White House

Union Station

NATIONAL MALL

Lincoln Memorial

U.S. Capitol

ARLINGTON NATIONAL CEMETERY

VIRGINIA

The Pentagon

Reagan Nat'l Airport

ANACOSTIA

Kenyon St.
Irving St.
Columbia Rd.
Harvard St.
Girard St.
Fairmont St.
Euclid St.

HOWARD UNIVERSITY

13th St. 12th St. 11th St. 10th St. 9th St. 8th St.

Barry Pl.

U STREET CORRIDOR

U STREET-CARDOZO

French St.

SHAW-HOWARD UNIVERSITY

Rhode Island Ave.

7th St. 6th St. 5th St. 4th St. 3rd St.

Florida Ave.

Logan Circle

29

1

13th St. 12th St. 11th St. 10th St. 9th St. 8th St.

N St.

M St.

New York Ave.

North Capitol St.

DOWNTOWN

MT. VERNON SQ./CONVENTION CTR.

50

1

K St.

New Jersey Ave.

Mt. Vernon Square

50

Massachusetts Ave.

395

I St.

New York Ave.

1

H St.

CHINATOWN

GALLERY PLACE-CHINATOWN

3rd St.

2nd St.

G St.

UNION STATION

METRO CENTER

12

F St.

E St.

11

JUDICIARY SQUARE

D St.

PENN QUARTER

Pennsylvania Ave.

C St.

Louisiana Ave.

Stanton Square

FEDERAL TRIANGLE

ARCHIVES-NAVY MEMORIAL

Constitution Ave.

13

Maryland Ave.

A St.

NATIONAL MALL

Madison Dr.

U.S. Capitol

CAPITOL HILL

East Capitol St.

SMITHSONIAN

Jefferson Dr.

14

A St.

Independence Ave.

Seward Square

North Carolina Ave.

L'ENFANT PLAZA

FEDERAL CENTER SW

Washington Ave.

New Jersey Ave.

CAPITOL SOUTH

Pennsylvania Ave.

EASTERN MARKET

Washington Channel

0   1/4 mi
0   0.25 km

395

South Capitol St.

See inset, above right

15

1. Hilton Washington
2. Woodrow Wilson House
3. 3321 Dent Place
4. 2808 P St
5. 3307 N St
6. Octagon Museum
7. Washington Monument
8. Star-Spangled Banner
9. Willard InterContinental
10. The Occidental
11. Ford's Theatre National Historic Site
12. National Portrait Gallery
13. Sewall-Belmont House
14. Library of Congress
15. Frederick Douglass National Historic Site
16. Lincoln's Cottage
17. Martin's Tavern

In the 21st century, America's capital city bears little resemblance to the swampy Potomac River Valley territory that President George Washington staked out as the new site for Congress in 1790. Yet trying to separate Washington from its past is like trying to take the red from blood. Because of its significance in U.S. history, Washington exists on two planes in the collective consciousness: first, as a real city with magnificent structures and whimsical cherry trees juxtaposed against a backdrop of still-recovering pockets of poverty; and second, as a virtual city of suspenseful Hollywood lore, with its Deep Throat–esque covert operations, war games, and congressional plottings. The true Washington lies somewhere between fact and fiction, past and present, and that is why it never loses its intrigue or its allure. You can modify this tour to fit your schedule and level of interest, but allow several days if you wish to visit every stop. START: **Metro to Smithsonian**

❶ ★★ **Hilton Washington.** In 1981, John Hinckley, Jr., an obsessed fan of actress Jodie Foster, ambushed Ronald Reagan here, just 69 days into the president's first term, in a misguided attempt to impress the star. Hinckley fired six shots, one of which struck Reagan's armpit. (Reagan's press secretary James Brady was also seriously injured; paralyzed from the waist down, he has been in a wheelchair ever since.) The Secret Service whisked Reagan away to a waiting hospital, where he underwent emergency surgery, making the now-legendary joke to his doctors: "I hope you're all Republicans." Despite being 70, the president recovered quickly—and went on to tackle other concerns, like the Cold War. ⏱ *30 min. 1919 Connecticut Ave. NW.* ☎ *202/483-3000. www.hilton.com. Metro: Dupont Circle.*

❷ **Woodrow Wilson House.** This final residence of Nobel Peace Prize winner and 28th president Woodrow Wilson has been preserved to celebrate the great man's "Washington years," from 1913 to 1924. It is where he returned to civilian life after his 8-year term

President Woodrow Wilson's original office desk.

President John F. Kennedy and Jacqueline Kennedy's former residence in Georgetown.

guiding Americans through World War I, giving women the right to vote, and launching the League of Nations (now known as the United Nations). He lived the last 3 years of his life at this grand brick house. Inside, tour his drawing room, kitchen, bedrooms, and garden. ⏱ *1 hr. See p 87.*

❸ 3321 Dent Place. If you are a JFK buff, you'll want to explore both the east and west villages of Georgetown—Wisconsin Avenue divides the historic neighborhood into two enclaves—to check out where the 35th president once lived, in some cases with his glamorous wife, Jackie, and their two children, Caroline and John, Jr. Between January and June 1954, 3321 Dent Place was the first residence of Senator and Mrs. Kennedy after their marriage in September 1953. ⏱ *10 min.*

❹ 2808 P St. After a stint in Virginia, the Kennedys moved back to Georgetown, to this tony address, where they lived from January to May 1957. ⏱ *10 min.*

❺ 3307 N St. JFK purchased this home and presented it to Mrs. Kennedy after the birth of their daughter, Caroline. From here, they moved to the White House on January 20, 1961. ⏱ *10 min.*

❻ Octagon Museum. The Octagon is one of the oddest-looking buildings in downtown D.C., and its history is just as intriguing. Built in 1799 for the Tayloe family, the building served as a temporary home to James and Dolley Madison after the White House was burned by the British in 1814. Ironically, the Treaty of Ghent, ending war with Great Britain, was signed on its second floor. The Octagon was also a girls' school and a tenement and is presently home to the American Architectural Foundation. ⏱ *1 hr. 1799 New York Ave. NW.* ☎ *202/626-7439. www.theoctagon.org. Open for self-guided audio tours Thurs–Fri, 1–4pm. Metro: Farragut West.*

❼ ★★ Washington Monument. In 1838, architect Robert Mills designed the largest—and perhaps most famous—masonry structure in the world, the 550-foot (168m) Washington Monument honoring George Washington. While it now resembles a solitary and unadorned Egyptian obelisk, Mills originally intended the marble shaft to rise from a circular building containing a huge statue of the first American president. After much bickering over its design, years of

The "star-spangled banner" that inspired the national anthem.

Martha Stewart's kitchen at the Museum of American History.

construction, and halted progress during the Civil War (which led to its two-tone marble effect, still visible today), the monument was finally completed and opened to the public on October 9, 1888. An earthquake in August 2011 shook the Monument so badly that trips to the top for spectacular views of the Mall are temporarily suspended; once it reopens in 2014, those dying to walk up and down its 897 steps can do so again, provided that they first contact the National Park Service at least a month in advance for a

guided tour. ⏱ *1 hr. 15th St. SW.* ☎ *202/426-6841, or 800/967-2283 (for reservations). www.nps.gov/wamo. Free timed tickets are available at the 15th St. kiosk on a first-come, first-served basis. Advanced tickets are available through the National Park Service. Tickets required for everyone 2 and up. Daily 9am–4:45pm. Closed July 4th and Dec 25. Metro: Smithsonian.*

❽ ★★★ **Star-Spangled Banner.** O, say can you see the garrison flag that has come to represent our coun-

Walk Through History

Cultural Tourism DC offers a series of guided and self-guided tours throughout the District. Bus tours include tailored itineraries for individual groups, planned in advance with CTDC; "anecdotal" history tours conducted by author/historian guide Anthony Pitch; neighborhood tours of U Street and Capitol Hill; even a city segway tour, on which—you guessed it—travelers sightsee on segways. Self-guided walking tours include the U Street Heritage Trail, where visitors follow numbered signs with information about this historic neighborhood; the Downtown Heritage Trail, which guides tourists though high and low points in D.C. history, from the Civil War through the Civil Rights era; and the Adams Morgan Heritage Trail, a walk through this vibrant community of artists, immigrants, and start-up entrepreneurs. To plan a specialized tour, sign up for a bus tour, or learn how to take a self-guided walking tour, visit www.culturaltourismdc.org.

try and its democratic ideals? You'll find it and its companion exhibit, "The Flag That Inspired the National Anthem," at the newly reopened National Museum of American History. Backstory: In 1814, Francis Scott Key peered through the clearing smoke after a 25-hour British bombardment of Baltimore's Fort McHenry and saw this very flag flapping proudly in the wind. He immediately wrote a poem that was set to music and sung at the country's patriotic events ever after. In 1907, the worn and tattered but powerfully symbolic flag was donated to the museum; in 1931, the song became our national anthem. After undergoing several years of preservation, the flag is now resting in its new high-tech atrium in the museum, designed to keep it carefully protected but still allow throngs of visitors to see this important American artifact. ⏱ *30 min. 14th St. and Constitution Ave. NW.* ☎ *202/633-1000. www.americanhistory.si.edu. Daily 10am–5:30pm (until 7:30pm in summer). Metro: Smithsonian and Federal Triangle.*

⑨ Willard InterContinental. Beaux-Arts architecture meets history at the formal, elegant Willard

InterContinental, which, at press time, had welcomed every president from Pierce through "W." It is the place where the Rev. Martin Luther King, Jr. wrote his legendary "I Have a Dream" speech. President Ulysses S. Grant held frequent meetings in the hotel lobby, and a host of celebrity visitors from Walt Whitman to P. T. Barnum have also overnighted here. Steven Spielberg even shot the final scene of *The Minority Report* with contemporary Hollywood heavyweight Tom Cruise here. It's worth ducking inside to admire the awe-inspiring lobby. *See p 166.*

Join in the weekday lunch rush at the **⑩** ★★ **Occidental,** adjacent to the Willard InterContinental, which welcomes a virtual who's who of Washington. Romantics yearn for the hotel's Jenny Lind Room, named for a racy 19th-century opera singer; the suite's elevated Jacuzzi sits below a large window that perfectly frames the Washington Monument in all its vertical glory. *1475 Pennsylvania Ave. NW (at 14th St.).* ☎ *202/783-1475. www.occidentaldc.com. $$$$. Metro: Metro Center.*

Booth's murder weapon.

A sculpture at the Sewall-Belmont House.

⓫ ★★ Ford's Theatre National Historic Site. Another shot heard round the world was fired here on April 14, 1865, when President Abraham Lincoln was killed as he watched a performance of *Our American Cousin.* The theater was immediately closed, and remained so for another 103 years. In 1968, it reopened as a living, working tribute to our late leader, serving as a functioning playhouse and a Lincoln repository for historic materials such as assassin John Wilkes Booth's Derringer pistol, the gun that killed the president. In 2006, the theater closed once again for renovations and reopened in early 2009, with an expanded museum on the president, plus a new lobby, box office, and seating. ⏱ *1½ hr., or more if you plan to see a show. 511 10th St. NW.* ☎ *202/347-4833.*

Mount Vernon

Easily accessible from the District, **George Washington's Mount Vernon Estate and Gardens,** 3200 Mount Vernon Memorial Hwy. (☎ **703/780-2000;** www.mountvernon.org), is 16 miles (26km) south of the capital. Educational and appealing to kids and adults alike, this impressive historic homestead is where the first president and his wife, Martha, lived from their wedding in 1759 until Washington's death 40 years later. Tour the main house and see Washington's library, the dining room and parlors, and the bedrooms. The plantation's outbuildings include the kitchen, smokehouse, storeroom, overseer's house, and the cramped slaves' quarters, a somber testament to a dark period in U.S. history. An on-site museum and visitors center has more than 500 artifacts from the Washington family, including furnishings, china, silver, clothing, jewelry—even Revolutionary War artifacts and rare books. Activities, from musical events to garden parties, take place year-round. To reach Mount Vernon, take the **Metro Rail Yellow Line** (☎ **202/637-7000;** www.wmata.com) to Huntington Station, Virginia. Exit at the lower level to catch a **Fairfax Connector** (☎ **703/339-7200**) bus no. 101 (Fort Hunt Line) for the 20-minute trip to Mount Vernon. Admission is $15 adults, $14 seniors, $7 kids 6 to 11, and free for kids 5 and under. The site is open to visitors April to August daily (8am–5pm), March and September to October daily (9am–5pm), and November to February daily (9am–4pm).

The Frederick Douglass National Historic Site, in Anacostia.

www.fordstheatre.org. Advance tickets $2.50. Limited number of free tickets available on first come, first served basis at 8:30am. Daily 9am–5pm, except Dec 25. Metro: Metro Center.

⑫ ★★★ National Portrait Gallery. While the building itself has a rich history—it served as the National Patent Office for 92 years—the Gallery's contents might be considered even more important. Some of the most treasured paintings, sculptures, and artifacts from American history are housed in this ode to its presidents, first ladies, and stars. See the original Gilbert Stuart portrait of George Washington, saved by Dolley Madison in the War of 1812, along with modern depictions of Richard Nixon, John F. Kennedy, and even Barack Obama. ⏱ *1 hr. 8th and F sts. NW.* ☎ *202/633-8300. www.npg.si.edu. Free admission. Daily, 11:30am–7pm, except Dec 25. Metro: Gallery Place/Chinatown.*

⑬ Sewall-Belmont House. Including the works and words of "radicals" such as Susan B. Anthony and Gloria Steinem, this museum traces the evolution of a revolution—the women's movement, in all of its fits, starts, and back-and-forward progress. Check out authentic picketing banners, 5,000 prints and photographs, original cartoons, more than 50 scrapbooks from early suffragists, paintings, sculptures, publications, and more. ⏱ *1 hr. By docent tour only. See p 99.*

⑭ ★ Library of Congress. Original presidential documents, plus photographs, multimedia, and more can be found at the Library of Congress, which houses the most comprehensive collection of archival material documenting this country's birth and growth as a nation. It occupies three adjacent buildings on Capitol Hill: the Thomas Jefferson Building (1897), the John C. Adams Building (1938), and the James Madison Building (1981). Docent-led, scheduled public tours depart Monday through Saturday, from the Great Hall of the Thomas Jefferson Building, at 10:30am, 11:30am, 1:30pm, 2:30pm, and 3:30pm. ⏱ *1 hr. Arrive 30 min. before tour begins. 101 Independence Ave. SE. www.loc.gov. Mon–Fri 9am–4:30pm, except federal holidays. Metro: Capitol South or Union Station.*

⑮ Frederick Douglass National Historic Site. Born a slave, Frederick Douglass escaped

Mount Vernon, the former home of President George Washington.

his circumstances to become, as President Lincoln once said, "the most meritorious man" of the 19th century. An outspoken abolitionist, a feminist, a human-rights pioneer, an ambassador, a minister, a family man, and the father of the Civil Rights movement, Douglass settled here in southeast D.C. at a home he called Cedar Hill, where his personal belongings are now on display. National Park Service rangers lead tours of the house, sharing the stories and legacy of this important American icon. ⏱ *1 hr. 1411 W St. SE.* ☎ *202/426-5961. Free admission. Daily Apr 1–Oct 31 9am–5pm; Nov 1–Mar 31 9am–4:30pm. Closed Jan 1, Thanksgiving, and Dec 25. Metro: Anacostia, then bus no. 2, which stops in front of the house.*

⑯ ★★ Lincoln's Cottage. When the sweltering heat of D.C. got to be too much for President Lincoln and his family, they retreated to this cottage, originally known as the Soldier's Home. Each June through November during 1862 to 1864, the Lincolns would take in the cool breezes from this house, on the third-highest area in Washington, 3 miles (5km) north of what was then downtown. After a restoration by the National Trust for Historic Preservation, this presidential landmark debuted to the public in 2008 and began offering 1-hour guided tours. The cottage is a straight shot up the Green Line on the Metro, and is well worth the detour if you can spare the time. ⏱ *2 hr. including commute. Rock Creek Church Rd. NW and Upshur St. NW.* ☎ *202-829-0436. Metro: Georgia Avenue/Petworth then taxi (to the Armed Forces Retirement Home campus, Eagle Gate entrance).*

Tuck into a booth at **⑰ Martin's Tavern** in Georgetown and you'll be transported to a time when Harry Truman, Lyndon Johnson, and even Richard Nixon regularly held court in the tiny pub. Opened in 1933 and still owned by the Martin family, it's a standby among locals for dinner and drinks. Don't miss the "proposal" booth, where JFK is rumored to have proposed to Jackie. *1264 Wisconsin Ave. NW;* ☎ *202/333-7370. www.martins-tavern.com. $–$$. No Metro Access. Cabs available on Wisconsin Ave.* ●

Africa

National Gallery of Art

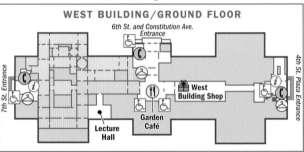

WEST BUILDING/GROUND FLOOR

6th St. and Constitution Ave. Entrance

7th St. Entrance

4th St. Plaza Entrance

West Building Shop

Garden Café

Lecture Hall

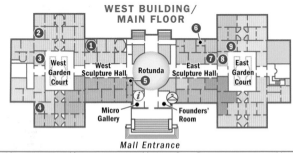

WEST BUILDING/MAIN FLOOR

❷ ❶ West Garden Court ❸ West Sculpture Hall ❻ Rotunda ❺ East Sculpture Hall ❼ ❽ East Garden Court ❾ ❹

Micro Gallery

Founders' Room

Mall Entrance

Constitution Ave. NW

Pennsylvania Ave. NW

9th St. NW

7th St. NW

Ice Rink

National Sculpture Garden

National Gallery of Art
(West Building)

Mall Entrance

4th St. NW

3rd St. NW

(East Building) ❿ ⓫ ⓬ ⓭ ⓮

Madison Dr. NW

NATIONAL MALL

❶ Leonardo's *Ginevra de' Benci* (Gallery 6)
❷ Raphael's *Saint George and the Dragon* (Gallery 20)
❸ El Greco's *Christ Cleansing the Temple* (Gallery 28)
❹ Velázquez's *The Needlewoman* (Gallery 34)
❺ Vermeer's *Woman Holding a Balance* (Gallery 50C)
❻ Monet's *Rouen Cathedral, West Facade* (Gallery 87)
❼ Monet's *Woman with a Parasol* (Gallery 85)
❽ Van Gogh's *Self Portrait* (Gallery 84)
❾ Gauguin's *Parau na te Varua ino* (Gallery 83)
❿ Calder's *Untitled* (East Bldg. Gallery 100 Ceiling)
⓫ Cascade Café (East Bldg. Concourse)
⓬ Picasso's *Nude Woman* (East Bldg. Upper-Level Gallery 404C)
⓭ O'Keeffe's *Jack-in-the-Pulpit No. 3* (East Bldg. Upper-Level Gallery 404E)
⓮ Pollock's *Number 1 (Lavender Mist)* (East Bldg. Concourse Gallery 29H)

🍴	Cafe
◒	Coat Room
ⓘ	Information
🎁	Museum Shop
☏	Telephone
♿	Wheelchair Accessibility

Previous page: A stuffed tiger at the Museum of Natural History in D.C.

ounded in 1937 by philanthropist Andrew Mellon with seed works from his personal collection, the National Gallery is one of the finest repositories of Western painting, sculpture, and graphic art on Earth. And, unlike most museums of its ilk, it's free to visitors. The collection ranges from revered early Renaissance paintings, including the only Leonardo da Vinci painting in the United States, to works by contemporary artists such as Ellsworth Kelly. You will recognize many a masterpiece as you make your way through the galleries, organized by school and arranged chronologically. The following itinerary features hallmark paintings of the collection. Plan to spend a couple of hours here; art lovers may want to linger an afternoon or a day. For more extensive coverage of modern and contemporary works, see "19th- & 20th-Century Art Museums" on p 72. START: **Metro to Archives, Judiciary Square, or Smithsonian**

Visitor viewing Ginevra de' Benci, *the best-preserved example of Leonardo da Vinci's early work.*

❶ Leonardo's *Ginevra de' Benci* (1474). Leonardo da Vinci's portrait of a wealthy young Florentine woman, one of the most esteemed intellectuals of her day, was probably commissioned by Venetian ambassador to Florence Bernardo Bembo, with whom the sitter had a platonic affair (an accepted Renaissance convention). The juniper plant (*ginepro* in Italian,

a pun on her name) symbolizes chastity, and the reverse side of the painting bears the motto "Beauty Adorns Virtue." *Gallery 6.*

❷ ★★ Raphael's *Saint George and the Dragon* (1506). Early Italian Renaissance painter Raphael created this work for the royal court of Urbino. In it, a Roman soldier of Christian faith subdues a dragon to

Practical Matters

The National Gallery (☎ **202/737-4215;** www.nga.gov) is located on the Mall between 3rd and 7th streets. Admission is free. It's open Monday through Saturday from 10am to 5pm and Sunday 11am to 6pm; closed December 25 and January 1.

Sculptures in the National Gallery.

save a pagan princess, whose survival inspires a mass conversion to Christianity among her subjects. *Gallery 20*.

③ El Greco's *Christ Cleansing the Temple* (1570). In this interpretation of the Protestant Reformation, the Spanish painter El Greco presents an angry Christ, emphasizing the widespread aggravation with the Catholic church's decisions at the time. His techniques for depicting space and three-dimensional figures were far more advanced than those of his Byzantine contemporaries, marking a turning point in his artistic career. *Gallery 28*.

④ Velázquez's *The Needlewoman* (1640). Spain's golden age of painting is best represented by the works of Diego Velázquez, one of the greatest masters of 17th-century Europe. The muted tones in this unfinished work show a departure from his earlier extreme contrasts of light and dark. *Gallery 34*.

⑤ Vermeer's *Woman Holding a Balance* (1664). With his characteristically delicate treatment of light, Dutch master Johannes Vermeer depicts a woman quietly going about her everyday work, her facial expression serene. Seventeenth-century Dutch paintings often focused on such themes, conveying the message that God's work was evident in the smallest or most inconsequential of details. *Gallery 50C*.

⑥ ★ Monet's *Rouen Cathedral, West Facade* (1894). Artists' obsessions with the Impressionist movement began to waver in the mid-1880s, when many, including Monet, broke away and began a series of paintings on one object. Here, Monet focuses on the Rouen Cathedral, of which he created more than 20 representations during his time spent in rented rooms across from it. This image reflects Monet's interest in light, texture, color, and mood. *Gallery 87*.

⑦ ★★★ Monet's *Woman with a Parasol* (1875). Impressionism would certainly win a recognition contest if pitted against other art movements, and Claude Monet just might take the prize for the most popular artist. This well-known painting demonstrates his mastery of light, landscape, and vibrant color. *Gallery 85*.

⑧ Van Gogh's *Self Portrait* (1889). One of 36 self-portraits from this prolific artist, this work is thought to have been produced in a single sitting without retouching. Van Gogh portrays himself at work, dressed as an artist. It is one of the last self-portraits he ever painted. *Gallery 84*.

⑨ Gauguin's *Parau na te Varua ino (Words of the Devil*; 1892). Paul Gauguin escaped to Tahiti and fell in love with its innocent, unspoiled culture.

His sense of paradise there—coupled with a biblical reference suggesting that Western civilization lost its chance at innocence and modesty with the fall of Adam and Eve—is evident in this classic nude painting. *Gallery 83.*

⑩ ★★★ Calder's *Untitled* (1976). In 1972, Calder began constructing this 76-foot-long (23m) mobile, commissioned specifically for the National Gallery's East Building. Installed in 1977, 1 year after his death, it was the artist's last major work of art. *East Building, Gallery 100 Ceiling.*

Enjoy views of a cascade waterfall while noshing on soups, salads, wood-fired pizzas, sandwiches, and fresh-baked desserts at the **⑰ Cascade Café.** *No phone. East Building Concourse. $.*

⑫ ★★★ Picasso's *Nude Woman* (1910). One of the most radical movements in art history can be attributed in part to Spanish painter Pablo Picasso, whose Cubist explorations with Georges Braque created a window to a new, fractured sense of space and time. *East Building, Upper-Level Gallery 404C.*

The Needlewoman, *by Diego Velázquez, at the National Gallery.*

⑬ ★★★ O'Keeffe's *Jack-in-the-Pulpit No. 3* (1930). Georgia O'Keeffe's sensuously abstracted flowers celebrate nature and make an overt nod to the female form. This painting, along with three others, was bequeathed to the Gallery by O'Keeffe herself. *East Building, Upper Level, Gallery 404E.*

⑭ ★★★ Pollock's *Number 1 (Lavender Mist; 1950).* Of his spontaneous, intuitive innovation—pouring paint directly onto unprimed canvas—Jackson Pollock once remarked, "There is no accident." *Lavender Mist* is one of the artist's most important drip paintings, in which his long, rhythmic movements are discernible. *East Building, Concourse Gallery 29H.*

Johannes Vermeer's Girl with the Red Hat, *at the National Gallery.*

National Museum of
Natural History

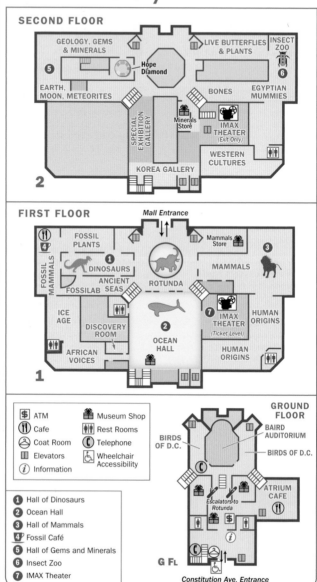

SECOND FLOOR

GEOLOGY, GEMS & MINERALS

LIVE BUTTERFLIES & PLANTS

INSECT ZOO

5

Hope Diamond

EARTH, MOON, METEORITES

BONES

EGYPTIAN MUMMIES

6

SPECIAL EXHIBITION GALLERY

Minerals Store

IMAX THEATER (Exit Only)

WESTERN CULTURES

KOREA GALLERY

2

FIRST FLOOR

Mall Entrance

FOSSIL PLANTS

Mammals Store

4

1

DINOSAURS

3

MAMMALS

FOSSIL MAMMALS

ANCIENT SEAS

ROTUNDA

FOSSILAB

ICE AGE

DISCOVERY ROOM

OCEAN HALL

2

IMAX THEATER (Ticket Level)

7

HUMAN ORIGINS

AFRICAN VOICES

HUMAN ORIGINS

1

$	ATM		Museum Shop
🍴	Cafe	🚻	Rest Rooms
	Coat Room	Ⓒ	Telephone
	Elevators	♿	Wheelchair Accessibility
ⓘ	Information		

1 Hall of Dinosaurs
2 Ocean Hall
3 Hall of Mammals
4 Fossil Café
5 Hall of Gems and Minerals
6 Insect Zoo
7 IMAX Theater

GROUND FLOOR

BIRDS OF D.C.

BAIRD AUDITORIUM

BIRDS OF D.C.

ATRIUM CAFE

Escalators to Rotunda

G Fl

Constitution Ave. Entrance

Kids go ape over this museum, "dedicated to understanding the natural world and our place in it." This vast repository houses thousands of natural relics, some of which date back millions of years. If you care to learn about global warming, African cultures, the social habits of insects, the Big Bang, or fossilized bones, you might end up wishing you'd devoted your entire trip to the largest of the Smithsonian Institution's 14 museums. Of the Smithsonian's 142 million objects, nearly 90%—that's 125 million artifacts—belong to this museum. Give yourself a minimum of an hour to explore this place. START: **Metro to Archives, Judiciary Square, or Smithsonian**

The National Museum of Natural History's Hope Diamond—the world's largest deep blue diamond, a billion-plus years old.

1 ★★ **Hall of Dinosaurs.** If you have young children, you might want to make your first stop the first-floor Discovery Room, which is filled with creative hands-on exhibits "for children of all ages." On the first floor, beyond the rotunda with its giant elephant, you'll find the real Jurassic Park, with its towering exhibitions of those fascinating, larger-than-life creatures from the distant past—the dinosaurs. The collection includes a giant Diplodocus and the complete skeleton of an Allosaurus (think T. Rex, only smaller).

Mounted throughout the Dinosaur Hall are replicas of ancient birds, including a life-size model of the *Quetzalcoatlus northropi,* which lived 70 million years ago, had a 40-foot (12m) wingspan, and was the largest flying animal ever. Also residing above this hall is the jaw of an ancient shark, the *Carcharodon megalodon,* which lived in the oceans 5 million years ago. A monstrous 40-foot-long (12m) predator with teeth 5 to 6 inches (13–15cm) long, it could have consumed a Volkswagen Bug in one gulp.

2 **Ocean Hall.** In late 2008, the museum debuted a brand-new, 22,000-square-foot (2,044-sq.-m) hall, the largest, most diverse exhibit of its kind in the world.

Practical Matters

The Museum of Natural History (☎ **202/633-1000;** www.mnh.si.edu) is located on the north side of the Mall, on Constitution Avenue NW between 9th and 10th streets. Admission is free. The museum is open daily from 10am to 5:30pm (until 7:30pm in summer; call ahead to confirm), except December 25.

A stuffed elephant greets visitors to the Museum of Natural History.

Designed by the same firm that created the exhibits and spaces of the highly interactive International Spy Museum, the hall includes collections and state-of-the-art technology to demonstrate our oceans' essential role in life on Earth. Look for ice age animals and loads of fossilized plants, among other preserved treasures. A model of a 45-foot-long (14m) North American right whale and a 1,500-gallon (5,678L) coral reef aquarium with more than 70 live animals and 674 specimens are also big hits.

❸ Hall of Mammals. This exhibit represents the "new" face of the museum: Set in the restored west wing, with up-to-date lighting and sound, it features interactive dioramas that explain how mammals evolved and adapted to changes in habitat and climate over millions of years. More than 270 stuffed mammals, including a polar bear and a lion, are on display, along with a dozen mammal fossils. From time to time, the hall erupts with animal sounds, all part of the curatorial wizardry that helps make your visit a lifelike experience.

Before heading up to the second floor, make a pit stop for a quick sandwich, snack, or even a cold one at the **❹ Fossil Café.** *No phone. First Floor, in Dinosaur Hall. $.*

Visitors observing gems at the National Museum of Natural History.

A T-Rex skeleton at the Museum of Natural History.

⑤ ★★★ Hall of Gems and Minerals. On the second floor, the Janet Annenberg Hooker Hall of Geology and Gems and Minerals features the infamous, cursed Hope Diamond. Legend has it that the rare blue diamond was originally stolen in the late 17th century, in its native India, from a statue of the Hindu goddess Sita. Following the incident, the object reputedly brought bad luck to anyone who claimed it. From nasty French royals Louis XVI and Marie Antoinette to a consortium of wealthy playboys and socialites, all either met untimely deaths or watched their dearest loved ones die badly—very badly. Jeweler Harry Winston purchased the gem in 1947 and immediately gave it to the museum, probably with more than a little relief. Here you can also learn all you want about earth science, from volcanology to the importance of mining. Interactive computers, animated graphics, and a multimedia presentation of the "big picture" story of the earth are among the features that have advanced the exhibit and the museum a bit further into the 21st century.

⑥ ★ Insect Zoo. Also on the second floor, those with an interest in creepy-crawlies can view live spiders, ants, millipedes, and centipedes up close, and learn what made the arthropods the animal kingdom's biggest grouping. Kids enjoy looking at tarantulas, centipedes, and the like, and crawling through a model of an African termite mound.

⑦ IMAX Theater. You just might jump out of your seat as nature's untamed beasts come barreling at you. Whether you are exploring the aliens of the deep oceans, taking a wild safari, or visiting Harry Potter's Hogwarts School of Wizardry, here you'll find the wonders of the world (and supernatural world) up close and at their most thrilling. Films rotate regularly; check the website to see what's playing during your visit.

A stuffed leopard from the Hall of Mammals, at the Museum of Natural History.

National Museum of **American History**

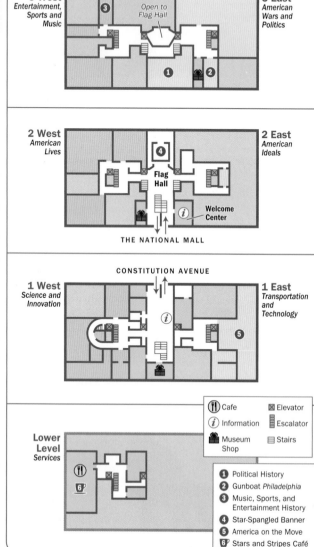

3 West
Entertainment, Sports and Music

❸

Open to Flag Hall

3 East
American Wars and Politics

❶   ❷

2 West
American Lives

❹

Flag Hall

Welcome Center

(i)

2 East
American Ideals

THE NATIONAL MALL

CONSTITUTION AVENUE

1 West
Science and Innovation

(i)

1 East
Transportation and Technology

❺

Lower Level
Services

🍴

❻

	Cafe	⊠	Elevator
(i)	Information		Escalator
🏛	Museum Shop	目	Stairs

❶ Political History
❷ Gunboat *Philadelphia*
❸ Music, Sports, and Entertainment History
❹ Star-Spangled Banner
❺ America on the Move
❻ Stars and Stripes Café

Calling all pop culture fans and American history buffs: This seriously entertaining Smithsonian museum is home to more than three million national treasures. Check out Dizzy Gillespie's angled trumpet, Dorothy's ruby red slippers, Julia Child's kitchen, and Muhammad Ali's boxing gloves. The original flag that inspired the national anthem is here, too, housed in a new high-tech gallery dedicated to its preservation. Plan to spend a few hours soaking up your fill of good ole Americana. START: **Metro to Smithsonian**

1 ★★ **Political History.** Throughout the museum, you'll find tons of artifacts, documents, and photographs celebrating the nation's political and presidential greats. The collection ranges from election campaign posters and ballots, to first ladies' clothing, to the personal effects of George Washington, Thomas Jefferson, and Abraham Lincoln. You'll see the top hat Lincoln wore on April 14, 1865, the night he was shot at Ford's Theatre; the cloth banner honoring the electoral victory of Thomas Jefferson over John Adams in 1800; and a Civil War surgical set. You'll also see more recent artifacts, such as a piece of the World Trade Center following the 9/11 attacks in 2001.

2 **Gunboat Philadelphia.** The only surviving gunboat from the Revolutionary War, the *Philadelphia* is now on view on the museum's third floor. One of eight identical ships constructed, it measures 53 feet (16m) long and 15 feet (4.5m) wide and was mounted with two

President Abraham Lincoln's famous top hat at the National Museum of American History.

cannons and numerous swivel guns. The *Philadelphia* was sunk in battle by the British in New York's Lake Champlain and remained at the bottom of the lake's Valcour Bay until 1935, when historians recovered it. The cold waters had kept its wood intact all those years, and it now rests here, along with the 24-pound (11kg) English cannonball that sent it to the bottom of the bay over 200 years ago.

3 ★★★ **Music, Sports, and Entertainment History.** Pop culture icons get a front-row seat at this museum. Even non-Hollywood buffs will appreciate *X-Files* memorabilia, Bruce Willis's T-shirts from *Die Hard* (he donated them to the museum in 2007), Archie Bunker's armchair from the popular (and controversial) sitcom *All in the Family*, the original Kermit the Frog puppet, and a Dumbo the Flying Elephant

Practical Matters

The National Museum of American History (☎ **202/633-1000;** www.americanhistory.si.edu) is located on the National Mall at 14th St. Admission is free. The museum is open daily from 10am to 5:30pm (until 7:30pm in summer), closed December 25.

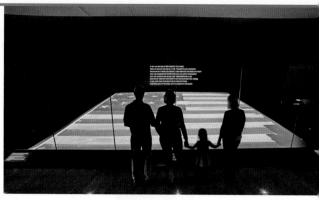

The Star-Spangled Banner *gallery at the Museum of American History.*

ride from 1955 Disneyland. An autographed Babe Ruth baseball; a 1989 Nintendo Gameboy; Julia Child's entire kitchen from her Cambridge, Massachusetts, home (donated part-and-parcel by the cook in 2001 when she moved residences); and the R2-D2 and C-3PO robots from the 1983 George Lucas blockbuster *Return of the Jedi* are just some more of the favorites found in this museum's vast collection.

❹ ★★★ *Star-Spangled Banner.* The British bombardment of Baltimore's Fort McHenry on September 14, 1814, lasted 25 hours,

but at its conclusion, this "flag was still there." The poignant sight of its battle-weary stripes and stars inspired Francis Scott Key to write *The Defence of Fort McHenry,* a poem that would eventually become the nation's National Anthem, titled *The Star-Spangled Banner.* The Smithsonian acquired the flag in 1907, and it has been undergoing restoration at the museum ever since. The exhibit was an integral part of the museum's recent renovation, and the nearly 200-year-old flag is now housed in a new, interactive gallery. The temperature and

The Gunboat Philadelphia *at the Museum of American History.*

lighting of the special chamber in which it lies are regulated to protect the 30 x 34 foot (9 x 10m) flag from further wear and tear, and the multi-story gallery with floor-to-ceiling glass windows is designed to give visitors a sense of the same "dawn's early light" that Key observed that morning in the harbor near Fort McHenry. The surrounding installation chronicles the story behind the flag's missing pieces, the Smithsonian's preservation efforts, and the national history that this artifact represents.

Vintage truck in the America on the Move exhibit at the Museum of American History.

5 ★ **America on the Move.** Do you still reminiscence about your first muscle car? It's likely represented here, along with a Chicago Transit Authority car, a 1903 Winton (the first car driven across the U.S.), a 92-foot-long (28m) Southern Railway locomotive, and even 40 feet (12m) of the American Southwest's renowned Route 66. Motor on down to the ground floor of the museum to see the nearly 20 life-size dioramas depicting America's transit history, from the first covered wagons that braved the Wild West to motor vehicles whose brethren still ply Route 66 and I-95 today. A range of some 300 artifacts—

including railway markers, signs, and photographs—are displayed in period settings to illustrate how America's railroad, canals, and roads changed the way its people traveled.

Tour the museum and then head to the aptly named **6** **Stars and Stripes Café** on the lower level for a culinary slice of Americana: basic soups, salads, burgers, pizza, and desserts. *No phone. $–$$.*

Southern Railway's 1401 steam locomotive, in the America on the Move exhibit at the Museum of American History.

19th- & 20th-Century Art Museums

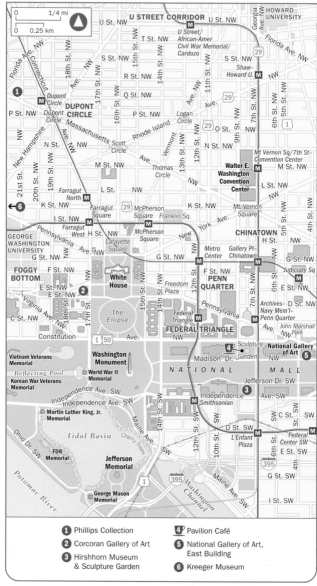

1 Phillips Collection
2 Corcoran Gallery of Art
3 Hirshhorn Museum & Sculpture Garden
4 Pavilion Café
5 National Gallery of Art, East Building
6 Kreeger Museum

In a world where what's considered current changes at an ever-faster pace—"That's, like, so 30 seconds ago!"—it's refreshing to view the art of the 1800s and 1900s, still thought of as modern, if not so subversive, well into the 21st century. It's also fun to put those art history classes to the test. START: **Metro to Dupont Circle (Q St. exit)**

1 Phillips Collection. The building that houses the Phillips Collection, widely considered America's first museum of modern art, was once the home of Duncan Phillips, grandson of the cofounder of the Jones and Laughlin Steel Company. The modern-looking newer wing generally shows fresh exhibitions; the museum also plays host to special lectures and tours. Some of its 2,472 artworks include Pierre-Auguste Renoir's *Luncheon of the Boating Party* (1880–81), Vincent van Gogh's *The Road Menders in Saint Remy* (1889), Edgar Degas's *Dancers at the Barre* (1884–88), and Georges Rouault's *Christ & the High Priest* (1937). ⏱ *1 hr. 1600 21st St. NW.* ☎ *202/387-2151. www.phillipscollection.org. Admission prices vary per exhibition. Tues–Sat 10am–5pm (Thurs to 8:30pm); Sun 11am–6pm (June–Sept to 5pm).*

2 ★★★ Corcoran Gallery of Art. Founded by William Wilson Corcoran, a "leading patron" of American art, the Corcoran contains a wildly varied selection of envelope-pushing contemporary art alongside 18th- and 19th-century masterworks. Here, you can admire *George Washington,* one of the legendary portraits by 18th-century artist Gilbert Stuart, and then walk a mere few steps away to analyze Andy Warhol's *Mao.*

Highlights include Edward Hopper's *Ground Swell* (1939), Edgar Degas's *The Dance Class* (1873), Jean-Baptiste-Camille Corot's *Repose* (1860), John Singer Sargent's *Mrs. Henry White* (1883) and *Setting Out to Fish* (1878), Frederic Remington's *Off the Range* (1902), and Mary Cassatt's *Young Girl at a Window* (1883). ⏱ *1 hr. 500 17th St. NW.* ☎ *202/639-1700. www.corcoran.org.*

Visitor viewing Renoir's famous Luncheon of the Boating Party *at the Phillips Collection.*

Louise Bourgeois's Crouching Spider *at the Hirshhorn Museum.*

Admission $10; $8 for students with ID, free for children; Thurs 5–9pm is pay what you wish. Wed–Sun 10am–5pm (Thurs until 9pm); closed Mon except holidays, Tues, Thanksgiving, Dec 25, and Jan 1.

❸ ★ **Hirshhorn Museum & Sculpture Garden.** First opened in 1974, the Hirshhorn Museum—built 14 feet (4.2m) aboveground on sculptured supports—is a unique vessel for a singular collection of modern and contemporary art. Amassed around Latvian émigré Joseph Hirshhorn's original donation of more than 9,500 works to the United States, the collection now includes art by Christo, Joseph Cornell, Arshile Gorky, and others. In the outdoor Plaza, visitors can gawk at the giant fountain and surreal sculptures. The Hirshhorn also has a sculpture garden across the street, with some 60 works of art. Other highlights of this eclectic outdoor exhibition are Emile-Antoine Bourdelle's *Great Warrior of Montauban* (1898–1900, cast 1956); Alexander Calder's *Stabile-Mobile* (1942) and *Deux Discs* (1965); Edward Hopper's *City Sunlight* (1954); Edgar Degas's *Dancer Putting on a Stocking* (1896); and Alberto Giacometti's *Walking*

Man II (1948). 🕐 *1 hr. Independence Ave. at 7th St. SW.* ☎ *202/633-4674. www.hirshhorn.org. Free admission. Daily 10am–5:30pm; plaza 7:30am–5:30pm, except Dec 25; sculpture garden 7:30am–dusk.*

The ❹ **Pavilion Café** is a cafeteria-style lunch spot that serves salads, veggie wraps, grilled meats, sandwiches, pizza, espresso drinks, and yummy baked goods near the National Gallery of Art Sculpture Garden. Dine outdoors on warm days, or admire the ice-skating rink on cold ones from within the cafe's cozy, family-friendly interior. *9th St. and Constitution Ave. NW (near Sculpture Garden).* ☎ *202/289-3360. $.*

❺ ★★★ **National Gallery of Art, East Building.** The trademarks of this 1978 I. M. Pei–designed building are its adjoining triangles of pink Tennessee marble (from the same quarry as the exterior of the neoclassical West Wing) that form sharp, acute angles at the corners. Inside, the centerpiece is the 76-foot-long (23m), 920-pound (417kg) mobile by Alexander Calder that hangs from the ceiling of the

Whistler at the Freer Gallery of Art

Founded by businessman Charles Lang Freer and opened to the public in 1923, the **Freer and Sackler Galleries of Art** are the very first Smithsonian museums for fine arts. They house a world-renowned collection of artworks from China, Japan, Korea, and Southeast Asia—as well as the largest collection of paintings by American artist James McNeill Whistler, who so famously produced a study of his mama in her rocking chair (*Whistler's Mother*, 1871). While Whistler's work may strike some as a bit out of place in a museum of Asian art, art lovers recognize how strongly influenced Whistler was by Japanese prints and Chinese ceramics. In fact, it was Whistler himself who, after befriending Freer in 1890, convinced the collector of primarily American works to begin buying art from the East, which Freer bequeathed to the museum. Whistler fans will be thrilled to learn that the Freer houses more than 1,300 paintings and drawings by this principal American artist. ⏱ *1½ hr. Jefferson Dr. at 12th St. SW.* ☎ *202/633-4880. www.asia.si.edu. Free admission. Daily 10am–5:30pm, except Dec 25.*

main atrium. Returned for display after restoration work, the mobile's construction includes aluminum tubing and aluminum honeycomb panels, which allow its arms to slowly and gracefully rotate. On the concourse hang nine color field paintings by Mark Rothko; with 295 paintings and more than 650 sketches, the National Gallery has one of the largest collections of Rothko artwork in the world. In the tower of the East Building are large "cutouts" by Henri Matisse, featuring beautiful colored shapes on large white backgrounds; it's one of the world's biggest collections of these works as well. ⏱ *1 hr. The National Mall, between 3rd and 7th sts. at Constitution Ave. NW.* ☎ *202/737-4215. www.nga.gov. Free admission. Mon–Sat 10am–5pm; Sun 11am–6pm; closed Dec 25 and Jan 1.*

❻ Kreeger Museum. This private museum is housed in the former residence of David and Carmen Kreeger, well-known collectors who amassed a sizable holding of 19th- and 20th-century paintings and sculptures. Highlights include works by Monet, van Gogh, Pissarro, Rodin, Kandinksy, and Cézanne. As you tour the museum, take note of its own modern architecture. Designed by architect Philip Johnson, it features a steel and concrete frame with glass walls and a free-form design. ⏱ *2 hr. including commute. 2401 Foxhall Rd. NW;* ☎ *202/337-3050, ext. 10. Tour reservations required (*☎ *202/338-3552). $10 adults; $7 students (with ID) and seniors over 65. Tues–Sat 10am–4pm. Closed Sun–Mon, the month of Aug. www.kreegermuseum.org. No Metro access.*

Special-Interest Museums

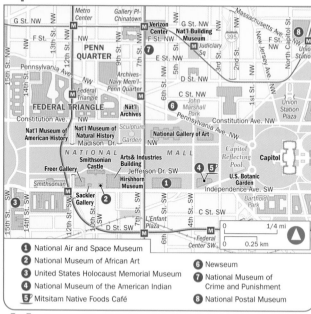

1. National Air and Space Museum
2. National Museum of African Art
3. United States Holocaust Memorial Museum
4. National Museum of the American Indian
5. Mitsitam Native Foods Café
6. Newseum
7. National Museum of Crime and Punishment
8. National Postal Museum

Maybe you fantasize about galaxies far, far away, or the spaceships that transport starry explorers. Perhaps you want to learn more about another ethnic group's art, culture, or history. Whatever your inclination may be, Washington, home to many renowned special-interest museums, can satisfy it. START: **Metro to L'Enfant Plaza or Smithsonian**

① ★★★ National Air and Space Museum. The most visited museum on the National Mall, this monument to avionics holds some 30,000 aviation artifacts and 9,000 space artifacts. The Wright Brothers' 1903 *Flyer*, the first successful powered airplane, is here, along with a reproduction of the original sketches for the machine. A complete collection of planes from World War II includes the famed Supermarine Spitfire Mk VII and a Mitsubishi A6M5 Zero, and Amelia Earhart's red *Lockheed Vega* (the one she flew solo across the Atlantic

Ocean in 1932). For those more interested in the stars, the National Air and Space Museum holds an original Apollo Lunar Module, one of 12 built for the program; astronaut and cosmonaut space suits; and, in one of the newest additions, Space-ShipOne, the first privately designed and built vehicle to reach space, and a harbinger of space tourism. It also houses the Lockheed Martin IMAX Theater, where you can explore the galaxies from the safety of your theater seat. ⏱ *1 hr. Independence Ave. at 6th St. SW.* ☎ *202/633-2214. www.nasm.si.edu. Free admission.*

Daily 10am–5:30pm (until 7:30pm in summer), except Dec 25.

2 National Museum of African Art. The only national museum solely dedicated to the acquisition, study, and exhibition of African art, this collection features both traditional and contemporary pieces, including everything from the spiritual (a Koranic writing board from Mali, an ivory pendant from the Congo) to the beautiful and practical (a carved wood fly whisk handle from Cote d'Ivoire). Ongoing exhibits include one focusing on African textiles: woven tapestries, robes, and clothes with particularly notable decorations and designs. Another exhibit features more than 140 contemporary and traditional ceramics from the continent. The museum also features regular music programs and tours. ⏱ *1 hr. 950 Independence Ave. SW.* ☎ *202/633-4600. www.nmafa.si.edu. Free admission. Daily 10am–5:30pm, except Dec 25.*

3 ★★ United States Holo-caust Memorial Museum. Be prepared to take an emotional journey when you enter this space, a living memorial to "never forgetting" the genocide of Europe's Jews, and the murder of all who opposed the rise of Germany's Nazi party, before and during World War II. Upon entering, you will be given (to keep) a faux passport of an actual Holocaust victim; some survived, but the great majority did not. The museum's centerpiece is its three-floor exhibit, entitled "The Holocaust." It's broken up into three subsections: "Nazi Assault," "Final Solution," and "Last Chapter." Through hundreds of artifacts and film footage, the story of one of humankind's biggest tragedies is laid out in exhaustive detail. The museum recommends that visitors be 11 years of age or older, due to the intensity of the

material. There is also a museum shop, a cafe, and the Wexner Learning Center on the second floor, where visitors can explore the survivors' registry and view materials about topics such as the Nuremberg Trials and the contemporary genocide emergency in Darfur. ⏱ *1 hr. 100 Raoul Wallenberg Place SW.* ☎ *202/488-0400. www.ushmm.org. Free admission, but from Mar–Aug, timed passes are necessary for visiting the permanent exhibition, and can be obtained at the museum on the day of your visit or in advance online. Each day, the museum distributes a large but limited number of timed-entry passes, on a first-come, first-served basis, for use that same day. Daily 10am–5:20pm, except Yom Kippur and Dec 25.*

4 ★★ National Museum of the American Indian. The newest big museum on the Mall is also one of the most distinctive, its exterior walls organically curved to sug-

The National Museum of the American Indian.

gest rock worn down by water. Dedicated to preserving the culture and history of Native Americans, the museum is also one of the most technologically advanced: Exhibits routinely incorporate video and other multimedia, including "Our Lives," which shows how Native American tribes live, striving to keep their ethnic identity, in contemporary times. ⏱ *1 hr. 4th St. and Independence Ave. SW.* ☎ *202/633-1000. www.nmai.si.edu. Free admission. Daily 10am–5:30pm, except Dec 25.*

On the first floor of the Museum of the American Indian, **5** **Mitsitam Native Foods Café** serves meals based on traditional Native American cuisines. *No phone. $–$$.*

6 ★★★ **Newseum.** All the news that's fit to print and more can be found in this seven-level high-tech monument to journalism. The history of news is told through interactive games and close-up views of hundreds of publications. Hear first-person accounts from reporters in the field, see a comprehensive collection of Pulitzer Prize–winning photojournalists' images, and discover the secrets to electronic news reporting. The "Be a Reporter" exhibit puts visitors in the hot seat: With a deadline looming and a breaking news story to report, grab a microphone and test your skills in front of the camera. How would you fare as the next Walter Cronkite? ⏱ *2 hr. 555 Pennsylvania Ave. NW.* ☎ *888/639-7386. www.newseum. org. Daily 9am–5pm, except Thanksgiving, Dec 25, and Jan 1. $22 adults, $18 seniors and students, $13 kids*

7–18, free for children 6 and under. Tickets good for 2 consecutive days. Metro: Archives/Navy Memorial.

7 **National Museum of Crime and Punishment.** CSI it's not, but this museum devoted to the history of crime is as close to a real-life experience as you can get (without all the danger). The hands-on exhibits outline the history of crime from the pillaging of pirates and medieval knights to the infamous Wild West outlaws Bonnie and Clyde. Exhibits include a full-scale model police station, a simulated FBI shooting range, and the actual television set of *America's Most Wanted.* Try your hand at cracking a safe or hacking into a computer and see if you could make it as a crook. ⏱ *1 hr. 575 7th St. NW.* ☎ *202/393-1099. www. crimemuseum.org. Hours vary by day and season. Check website for more details. $20 adults, $15 children, $17 seniors and military. Metro: Gallery Place/Chinatown.*

8 **National Postal Museum.** Calling all stamp collectors: Nirvana awaits you right next door to Union Station. One of the world's largest stamp collections resides at this ode to the U.S. Mail Service, established in 1886. Listen to tales of the early Pony Express and browse a vast assortment of historical postage dating back to the nation's infancy, plus international stamps, the first piece of correspondence to be flown across the Atlantic, and some original 24-cent inverted stamps. ⏱ *1 hr. 2 Massachusetts Ave. NE.* ☎ *202/633-5555. www.postalmuseum.si. edu. Free admission. Daily 10am–5:30pm, except Dec 25. Metro: Union Station.* ●

PERRYS
SPECIALS
SOFT SHELL CRAB
NY STRIP STEAK
UNI & YUZU JELLY
WHITE TUNA ROLL
TUNA 6 WAYS

Adams Morgan

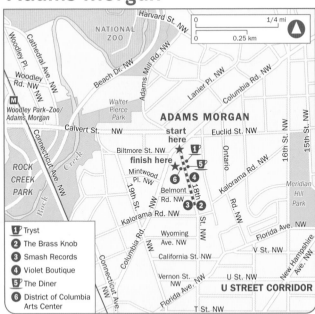

1. Tryst
2. The Brass Knob
3. Smash Records
4. Violet Boutique
5. The Diner
6. District of Columbia Arts Center

If you love New York's East Village, you'll feel right at home in this neighborhood, which is all about youthful verve, bohemian values, diversity, and a thriving street scene. Concentrate your explorations on 18th Street and the intersecting Columbia Avenue where you'll discover authentic ethnic restaurants, girlie boutiques, funky lounges, coffeehouses with sidewalk seating, and young people on display in their various rebellious uniforms. START: **Metro to Woodley Park–Zoo/Adams Morgan**

1 ★★ **Tryst** is one of those coffeehouses whose regulars seem to live in the place—you almost expect to find Ross, Rachel, Joey, and the gang camped out in the corner. A bar, a lounge, a diner, and a cafe, it shelters students doing homework; writers on their laptops; artists hanging their work for sale; and mohawked 8-year-olds running around, pastries in hand. Opens very early, closes very late. See p 148.

2 **The Brass Knob.** Looking for vintage decorative wares or the perfect stained-glass accent for your home? Look no further than this funky shop featuring one-of-a-kind objects from the 1800s to the early 1900s. You'll need plenty of time to peruse the store, filled with items such as antique chandeliers, iron

Previous page: Strolling through Adams Morgan.

gates, and columns, down to the smallest doorknob. 🕐 *30 min. 2311 18th St. NW.* ☎ *202/332-3370. www.thebrassknob.com. Mon–Sat 10:30am–6pm; Sun noon–5pm. Metro: Woodley Park/Adams Morgan.*

③ Smash Records. Spend an hour perusing the vinyl records, vintage clothing, and punk rock CDs found in this hole-in-the-wall shop in the heart of Adams Morgan. If you love records, you won't leave empty-handed. 🕐 *30 min. 2314 18th St., NW, 2nd Floor.* ☎ *202/38-SMASH (76274). www.smashrecords. com. Hours vary. Metro: Woodley Park Zoo (then 30-min. walk).*

④ Violet Boutique. A variety of affordable styles and accessories, plus super-friendly and knowledgeable owner Julie Egermayer, have made this funky shop on the main drag of Adams Morgan a go-to for fashionistas. 🕐 *30 min. 2439 18th St. NW.* ☎ *202/621-9225. www. violetdc.com. Tues–Fri noon–8pm; Sat 11am–8pm; Sun 11am–6pm. Closed Mon. Metro: Woodley Park–Zoo/Adams Morgan.*

The streets of Adams Morgan are lined with shops and hip cafes.

A mural in Adams Morgan.

⑤ The Diner purports to offer something for everyone, and it lives up to this claim with a full menu of salads, sandwiches, breakfast all day, and some of the best milkshakes in the city. You'll feel recharged after visiting this casual neighborhood fixture in the heart of Adams Morgan. *2453 18th St. NW.* ☎ *202/232-8800. www.dinerdc. com. Metro: Woodley Park/Adams Morgan*.

⑥ District of Columbia Arts Center. Adams Morgan is one of D.C.'s most eclectic neighborhoods, so where else would you find a funky art gallery and 50-seat theater among bars and restaurants that cater to the college scene? The nonprofit DCAC features up-and-coming artists in an intimate theater space, while the 750-sq.-foot (70-sq.-m) gallery spotlights a revolving calendar of innovative works. 🕐 *1½ hr. 2438 18th St. NW.* ☎ *202/462-7833. www.dcartscenter.org. Wed–Sun 2–7pm. Metro: Woodley Park–Zoo/ Adams Morgan.*

U Street Corridor/14th Street

1 Commissary DC

2 The Galleries on 14th Street

3 Miss Pixie's

4 Home Rule

5 Pulp DC

6 Greater U Street Heritage Trail

7 Lincoln Theatre

8 Ben's Chili Bowl

9 African American Civil War Memorial and Museum

10 Howard University

The riots of 1968—ignited by the assassination of Martin Luther King, Jr.—subjected the Corridor to 3 days of looting and devastation. Once known as the grand and glorious "Black Broadway," the strip was a shadow of its former self for decades afterward, better known for its crack houses than for its theater companies. Fourteenth Street, which intersects historic U Street and runs north to south, was also decimated during the riots. But new signs of life appeared in the late 1990s in both of these areas: A frenzied real-estate boom brought homesteaders to the neighborhood, and the requisite art galleries, trendsetting boutiques, scene-making cafes, and happening restaurants followed. It's best to start this walk after noon: No early opening hours here. START: **Metro to Dupont Circle**

Kick off your day with breakfast at **1 Commissary DC,** a cozy restaurant with outdoor tables that serves fantastic food three meals a day. Food runs the gamut from delicious omelets to tuna melts and a fish fry. If you're lucky, snag a comfy chair up front with pullout trays. It'll feel like dining in your living room, only much better. *1443 P St. NW. (btw. N. 14th St. & N. 15th St.).* ☎ *202/299-0018. www.commissary dc.com. Breakfast, lunch, and dinner daily. Metro: Dupont Circle.*

Café St.-Ex is a popular stop on the microbrewed beer circuit.

② The Galleries on 14th Street. Explore D.C.'s emerging contemporary art scene at this consortium of independent galleries. Begin your crawl at 1515 14th St. NW, which houses several talk-of-the-town galleries: **G Fine Art** (☎ 202/462-1601; www.gfineartdc. com), **Hemphill Fine Arts** (☎ 202/234-5601; www.hemphillfinearts. com), **Adamson Gallery** (☎ 202/232-0707; www.adamsongallery. org), and **Curator's Office** (☎ 202/387-1008; www.curatorsoffice. com). Then check out **Transformer,** 1404 P St. NW (☎ 202/483-1102; www.transformerdc.org) and **Gallery plan b,** down the block at 1530 14th St. NW (☎ 202/234-2711; www.galleryplanb.com). ⏲ *2 hr.* Metro: Cardozo/U St.

③ Miss Pixie's. Even if you don't think you need it, you'll still have to have it when you encounter this funky shop's eclectic collection of antiques, odd trinkets, and one-of-a-kind furniture cobbled from estate sales. The inventory rotates, so artful bookcases and retro chairs might be there one week and gone the next. ⏲ *30 min. 1626 14th St. NW. (between N. R St. & N. Corcoran St.).* ☎ *202/232-8171. www.misspixies. com. 11am-7pm daily. Metro: U Street/Cardozo*

④ Home Rule. Need a milk frother, stainless steel martini shaker, or a pair of "pot-holder dogs" (oven mitts that look like your mutt)? Of course you do! Look no further than this culinary-themed outpost for creative, colorful kitchen and bar accessories. ⏲ *30 min. 1807 14th St. NW (at S St.).* ☎ *202/797-5544. www.homerule.com. Mon–Sat 11am–7pm; Sun noon–5:30pm. Closed holidays. AE, DISC, MC, V. Metro: Cardozo/U St.*

⑤ Pulp DC. This cozy card store has a little something for everyone: gag gifts, stationery, fun totes, mugs, books, and candy. This D.C. mainstay of over 10 years is a one-stop shop for tchotchkes and irreverent knickknacks. ⏲ *30 min. 1803 14th St. NW.* ☎ *202/462-7857. www.pulpdc.com.*

⑥ ★★ Greater U Street Heritage Trail. As you explore this

Funky kitchenware at Home Rule.

section of town—the former home of Duke Ellington and the vital heart of African-American culture in the capital—you might notice 14 poster-size signs, with historical images and compelling stories. Follow these visual cues for a 90-minute, self-guided tour of historic U Street. The first sign is at 13th and U streets NW, near the Cardozo/U Street Metro stop; each sign will direct you to the next. Highlights include the Thurgood Marshall Center for Service and Heritage (home to the first African-American YMCA), the Whitelaw Hotel (the segregated capital's first luxury hotel for African Americans), the revived Bohemian Caverns (where the Ramsey Lewis Trio recorded the album "In Crowd"), and the restored Lincoln Theatre. Walkers are encouraged to follow the trail at their own pace, sampling neighborhood character, businesses, and restaurants along the way. For more information, a timeline of historical U Street events and vintage photographs, stop in the Greater U Street Neighborhood Visitor Center, located at the start of the trail near the Cardozo/U Street Metro stop. ⏱ 1½ hr. 1211 U St. NW. ☎ 202/661-7581. www.culturaltourismdc.org (click on "Tours & Trails"). Daily 10am–6pm.

7 ★ Lincoln Theatre. The jewel of what was once called "Black Broadway," the Lincoln hosted the likes of Ella Fitzgerald and Cab Calloway before desegregation. The theater went dark in 1979 but reopened 15 years later and was eventually restored to its original 1920s splendor. Today, it books jazz, R & B, gospel, and comedy acts—even events such as the D.C. Film Festival. ⏱ 1½ hr., or more if you plan to see a show. 1215 U St. NW. ☎ 202/397-SEAT (397-7328). For tours: 202/328-6000, ext. 220. www.thelincolntheatre.org. Tickets $20–$200. Metro: Cardozo/U St.

Open since 1958, **8 ★★ Ben's Chili Bowl** is a Washington institution. If this old-time diner's walls could talk, they would speak volumes about notable figures such as Martin Luther King, Jr.; Redd Foxx; Bill Cosby; and others who've sat at the Formica tables here. You just might catch a celebrity inhaling a Chili Half-Smoke—a quarter-pound half pork/half beef smoked sausage smothered in chili, of course—with a side of chili fries and an iced tea. **Tip:** Ben's is cash-only, but they have an ATM in back in case you get caught short. 1213 U St. NW. ☎ 202/667-0909. www.benschilibowl.com. $. Metro: Cardozo/U St. For sit-down dining, a bar, and expanded menu, head to the new Ben's Next Door. 1211 U St. NW. ☎ 202/667-8880. www.bensnextdoor.com. $$. Metro: Cardozo/U St.

9 ★ African American Civil War Memorial and Museum. This museum uses photography, audiovisual presentations, and historical documents and artifacts to

Ben's Chili Bowl.

One of the rare photos at the African American Civil War Museum.

commemorate the estimated 228,000-plus African-American soldiers and sailors who fought, largely unheralded, in the U.S. Civil War. Unveiled in 1998, the "Spirit of Freedom" sculpture, 2 blocks away, honors the sacrifices made by black soldiers and their families during the war. Designed by Ed Hamilton, of Louisville, Kentucky, it is also the first major artwork by an African-American sculptor to reside on federal land in the capital. ⏱ *45 min. 1925 Vermont Ave. NW at U St.* ☎ *202/667-2667. www.afroamcivil war.org. Free admission. Tues–Fri 10am–6:30pm; Sat 10am–4pm; Sun noon–4pm. Metro: Cardozo/U St.*

🔟 **Howard University.** Established in 1867 by a charter of the U.S. Congress, this educational institution was named after General Oliver Howard, a Civil War hero and commissioner of the Freedman's Bureau, which was instrumental in providing funds for the upstart university. Howard U. has come to be a bastion for the liberal and scientific arts, attracting the nation's best and brightest African-American students and other students of color, who are proud to continue the legacy of a school so involved in the Civil Rights movement of the 1960s. Current enrollment hovers near 11,000, with more than 7,000 undergraduates. Famous alumni include Thurgood Marshall, Debbie Allen, Sean "P. Diddy" Combs, Marlon Wayans, and Roberta Flack. ⏱ *20 min. 2400 6th St. NW.* ☎ *202/806-6100. www. howard.edu. Metro: Cardozo/U St.*

Stately, historic Howard University.

Dupont Circle

1. Kramerbooks & Afterwords Café
2. Phillips Collection
3. Woodrow Wilson House
4. Dupont Memorial Fountain
5. Circa
6. Lou Lou
7. Blue Mercury
8. Betsy Fisher
9. National Geographic Explorer's Hall
10. Hank's Oyster Bar
11. Eighteenth Street Lounge

Capitol Hill and the Mall may represent Washington to the world, but for locals, Dupont Circle is the heart of the District—a central point for meeting, lunching, strolling, shopping, and people-watching. Famous for its gay-friendliness, it's just plain old friendly to everyone, including visitors. Be sure to sit on a bench, rest your feet, and watch the world go by within the Circle itself, and ogle the master artworks at Duncan Phillips' private-home-turned-museum, The Phillips Collection (see below). For a nice mix of retailers, restaurants, bars, and clubs, check out Connecticut Avenue and nearby 17th Street. START: **Metro to Dupont Circle**

① ★★ **Kramerbooks & Afterwords Café.** Is it a restaurant? A bookstore? A coffeehouse? Open early and late (all night on weekends), it's the perfect spot to chat over lattes, browse bestsellers, grab a quick sandwich, and people-watch the Washingtonians who flock here in droves. The outdoor tables are at a premium in good weather, and weekend brunch is a popular time

to rendezvous with friends. ⏱ *1 hr. 1517 Connecticut Ave. NW.* ☎ *202/ 387-1400. www.kramers.com. $$. Opens very early; closes very late. Metro: See Start, above.*

② ★★ **Phillips Collection.** Before leaving Dupont Circle for points north, make a stop at the original home of renowned art collector Duncan Phillips. On opening his personal collection to the public in 1921, he established America's first modern art museum. His collection is still on view, and the museum remains one of the most popular in the District. Rooms in this historic brownstone feature works by Picasso, Degas, van Gogh, and O'Keeffe, along with several contemporary artists. Auguste Renoir's *Luncheon of the Boating Party* occupies an entire wall on the museum's second floor, and is the Phillips' most celebrated piece. ⏱ *2 hr. 1600 21st St. NW.* ☎ *202/387-2151. www. phillipscollection.org. Admission varies. Metro: Dupont Circle*

③ ★ Woodrow Wilson House.
Tour the former home of the 28th president, preserved as it was when he lived here during his final years in the 1920s. Docents guide visitors on hour-long tours of the Georgian Revival–style building, pointing out objects d'art, such as the French Gobelin tapestry given to Wilson by the French ambassador, and telling stories about our 28th president (such as the fact that he liked to whistle the tune "Oh You Beautiful Doll" to his beloved wife, Edith). You'll see Wilson's movie projector

President Woodrow Wilson's radio microphone.

in the library (he was a film buff); the typical 1920s kitchen, with one of the nation's first electric refrigerators; and Wilson's office, which his family called "the dugout." Office treasures include a baseball given to him at an Army-Navy game he attended with England's George VI. Upstairs, on his bedside table, lies *Imitation of Christ*, by Thomas à

Come to browse books, then snag a table for al fresco dining at Kramerbooks & Afterwords Café.

The iconic fountain at Dupont Circle was designed by Daniel Chester French and Henry Bacon and installed in 1921.

Kempis. See also "Historic Washington" on p 50. 🕐 *2 hr. 2340 S St. NW. ☎ 202/387-4062. www.woodrow wilsonhouse.org. $10 adults, $8 seniors, $5 students. Tues–Sun 10am–4pm; closed major holidays. Metro: Dupont Circle.*

❹ **Dupont Memorial Fountain.** A trip to Dupont Circle will undoubtedly include a stroll through this urban park, from which the neighborhood radiates in all directions. A giant marble statue of three classical figures representing sea, wind, and sky anchors the circular area that attracts dog walkers, musicians, bookworms, and lunchbreakers. Designed by Daniel Chester French—sculptor of the seated Abraham Lincoln at the Lincoln Memorial—and erected in 1921, it was placed on the National Register of Historic Places in 1978. 🕐 *20 min. Connecticut Ave. and New Hampshire Ave. NW. Metro: Dupont Circle.*

Sit outside at Dupont's ❺ **Circa** and watch the city go by while enjoying lobster ravioli, pear salads, and more than 20 wines by the glass. *1601 Connecticut Ave. NW. ☎ 202/667-1601. www.circaat dupont.com. $. Metro: Dupont Circle.*

❻ **Lou Lou.** Need a new belt for the night out? How about a new set of earrings? This charming boutique in the heart of Dupont Circle has more accessories than you'll ever need—hats, headbands, belts, scarves, jewelry, and bags—all at a very reasonable price. 🕐 *30 min. 1601 Connecticut Ave. NW. ☎ 202/ 588-0027. www.loulouboutiques. com. Mon–Sat 10am–8pm; Sun 11am–6pm. $. Metro: Dupont Circle.*

❼ **Blue Mercury.** This regional skin care, cosmetics, and bath shop has a beautiful clientele—women and men who can't buy enough of the store's Shu Uemera, Fresh, Decleor, and Paula Dorp product lines. Limited spa and beauty treatments are also available. 🕐 *20 min. 1619 Connecticut Ave. NW. ☎ 202/ 462-1300. www.bluemercury.com. Mon–Sat 10am–8pm; Sun 11am– 6pm. AE, DISC, MC, V. Metro: Dupont Circle or Farragut North.*

❽ ★★ **Betsy Fisher.** In a world where so many of us can spot our own outfits on others, it's nice to find a boutique with unique, fashion-forward apparel, shoes, and accessories for women—not girls—that are modern without being trendy. It's a good place to grab some basic accessories, too—think belts, boots, shoes, and bags. 🕐 *30 min. See p 108.*

❾ ★★ **kids** **National Geographic Explorer's Hall.** If you or your little ones are fans of world travel, space exploration, or both—or if you've been a reader of *National Geographic* all your life and simply want to see where the magazine is put together—this museum is a must-visit. Check out the society's rotating exhibits related to exploration, adventure, world cultures, and earth sciences, which incorporate interactive programs and artifacts. Conclude your expedition with a stop by the gift shop, whose ample collection of toys, gadgets, and gear will amuse your whole scouting party. ⏱ *1 hr. 17th and M sts. NW.* ☎ *202/857-7588. www.nationalgeographic.com/ museum. $8 adults, $6 seniors, $4 kids (5-12). Daily 10am–6pm. Closed Dec 25. Last tickets sold at 5:15pm. Tickets available online or in advance at 202/857-7700. Metro: Farragut N. (Connecticut Ave. and L St. exit).*

If your ideal evening (or afternoon) involves beer and oysters, you will find no better place than 🍵 ★★ **Hank's Oyster Bar.** This casually sophisticated, modern restaurant caters to low-key diners with a taste

Hank's Oyster Bar.

for fresh seafood. *1624 Q St. NW.* ☎ *202/462-4265. www.hanksdc. com. $$. Metro: Dupont Circle.*

Whether you arrive early in the evening to rest your feet as you sip a cocktail and sit, salon-style, on a sofa, or you show up late to listen to a live band with all the beautiful people, the legendary 🍵 **Eighteenth Street Lounge** is all about mingling, chilling to music, and posing pretty. *See p 151.*

Brass sculpture at the National Geographic Society's Explorer's Hall.

Georgetown

1 Evermay
2 Oak Hill Cemetery
3 Montrose Park
4 Tudor Place
5 Urban Chic
6 Georgetown University
7 Cady's Alley
8 Serendipity 3
9 C&O Canal
10 Old Stone House
11 Bourbon Steak

No visit to Washington is complete without a trip to historic and hip Georgetown—which somehow manages to balance frenzied consumerism with cultural relevance. For some of the neighborhood's most visited attractions, check out "The Best of D.C. in One Day," on p 8. Here are a few additional points of interest, high-end restaurants, and outstanding retailers. START: **Bus no. 30, 32, 34, 35, 36, or 38B to Thomas Jefferson and M streets**

1 ★★ **Evermay.** Built between 1792 and 1794, one of Georgetown's greatest mansions had an original owner who was both eccentric and obsessed with privacy. He went so far as to advertise dire predictions (bordering on threats) in the daily papers, warning the curious of trespassing on his property. Today it's privately owned, so you still can't tour the grounds, but you can steal a look through the iron gates. ⏱ *30 min. 1623 28th St. NW. No Metro access (see "Traveling to Georgetown," at right).*

2 **Oak Hill Cemetery.** This historic cemetery is just a short walk uphill from the shops of Georgetown's M Street. One of the oldest cemeteries in the city, it was established in 1849 and now holds the remains of many famous Washingtonians: Senators, Civil War generals, artists, designers, and Philip Graham, longtime publisher of the *Washington Post,* are all buried here. Among the grounds' great buildings and monuments are the Van Ness Mausoleum and Renwick

Tudor Place, a massive Georgetown mansion.

Chapel, designed by James Renwick, Jr., architect of the Smithsonian Building. ⏱ *30 min. 30th and R sts. NW.* ☎ *202/337-2835. www.oakhill cemeterydc.org. Mon–Fri 9am–4pm; Sun 1–4pm; closed to the public during funerals. Metro: Foggy Bottom.*

❸ ★ **Montrose Park.** Right next door to Oak Hill, Montrose was founded as a place "for the recreation and pleasure of the people." Rope-making tycoon Robert Parrott claimed the land in the early 1800s, and by the early 1900s, it had become the premier spot in town for picnics and leisurely strolls.

Street noises are so muffled, you might even feel you've left the city. ⏱ *45 min. On the block of 3000 R St. NW, next to Dumbarton Oaks. Open daily until dusk. No Metro access (see box, below).*

❹ ★ **Tudor Place.** One of the longest blocks in Georgetown is the stretch between Q and R streets on 31st Street NW. In a neighborhood where even the rich and famous get dog-eat-dog over square footage, it doesn't get more impressive than this estate, which sprawls nearly a full square block. This 1816 mansion was home to Martha Washington's granddaughter and her descendants

Traveling to Georgetown

Georgetown is not exactly convenient to reach. There are no Metro stops here, or even close to here; you will need to rely on bus or taxi transport for access. If you don't mind a walk, however, get off the Metro at either Foggy Bottom in D.C. or at Rosslyn, the first stop in northern Virginia (both are on the Blue and Orange lines), and hike 15 to 20 minutes. Foggy Bottom is a simple stroll west on Pennsylvania, which merges into M Street, Georgetown's main drag. Rosslyn is just across Key Bridge; traverse it and you're at the other end of Georgetown—perfect for a stop at Dean & Deluca for a snack. For bus schedules, check out www.wmata.com.

Georgetown University.

until 1984. ⏱ *30 min. 1644 31st St. NW. ☎ 202/965-0400. www.tudor place.org. Admission $8 adults, $6 seniors, $3 students. No reservations necessary for groups of 10 or less. Garden tours Mon–Sat 10am–4pm; house tours by docent only. No Metro access (see box, p 91).*

⑤ ★ Urban Chic. Not so long ago, D.C. was all about pearls and twinsets but, thank goodness, times have changed. This boutique is where the district's trendsetters select high-end denims; cool looks from Chloe, Marc Jacobs, and other designers; and saliva-inducing accessories, from wide belts to embellished earrings. ⏱ *20 min. See p 110.*

⑥ ★★★ Georgetown University. Like Harvard, Princeton, and Brown, Georgetown University evokes images of ivy-covered buildings, historic colleges, polo-wearing students, and academic types with furrowed brows appearing from their ivory towers. The campus grounds do not disappoint, from the architecture to the soccer pitch, and make for a lovely stroll on a nice day. Because the university is in the heart of Georgetown just a hop, skip, and jump from M Street's main drag (west of Wisconsin), the curious should not hesitate to tour it. (Look for the nearby *Exorcist* stairs, too, which were featured in a climactic

scene in the 1973 horror film, and connect the campus to M St. from Prospect St.) Founded by Father John Carroll (an appointed superior of the American Mission by the pope in 1784), the school officially opened its doors for study in 1789. More than 2 centuries later, the school is a top draw for continuing education, and boasts formidable alums such as President William Jefferson Clinton, and yes, the guy who wrote *The Exorcist,* William Peter Blatty. ⏱ *30 min. 37th and O sts. NW. ☎ 202/687-0100. www.georgetown.edu. No Metro access (see box, p 91).*

⑦ ★★ Cady's Alley. Looking for that perfect armchair to go with your new lamp? You'll likely find it here in D.C.'s design district. Sidled next to the C&O Canal in Georgetown, this cluster of shops features international and local contemporary furnishings and accessories. Artefacto, Contemporaria, and Ligne Roset are just a few of the purveyors you'll find in this lofty design center. ⏱ *1 hr. 3318 M St. NW (btw. 33rd and 34th sts.). www. cadysalley.com. Store hours vary. Metro: Foggy Bottom or Rosslyn.*

After a few hours of touring Georgetown, head to the venerable sweets restaurant **⑧ Serendipity 3** for a quick lunch break—or spring for the

$1,000 Golden Opulence, the most expensive ice-cream sundae in the world. *3150 M St. NW. ☎ 202/333-5193. www.serendipity3dc.com. $. No Metro access.*

⑨ C&O Canal. Perfect for families, this 185-mile (298km) waterway would take you to Cumberland, Maryland, if you were to follow its course. Stroll along the towpath, past historic homes and original canal locks. ⏱ *2 hr. 1057 Thomas Jefferson St. NW. ☎ 202/653-5190. www.nps.gov/choh. Admission $8 adults, $6 seniors, $5 children 4–14, free for children 3 and under. Mid-Apr to late Oct Wed–Sun 9am–4:30pm. No direct Metro access (Metro to Foggy Bottom is a 15-min. walk). Bus: See Start, above.*

⑩ ★ Old Stone House. On M Street—between modern attractions like Sephora and Hu's Shoes—is the Old Stone House, one of the capital's oldest buildings, built in 1765. Give your credit card a rest; explore its interior, and learn how Washingtonians lived nearly 250 years ago. ⏱ *30 min. 3051 M St. NW.*

Shoppers on M St.

☎ 202/895-6070. www.nps.gov/olst. Free admission. Daily noon–5pm. No Metro access. See box, p 91.

The chic and contemporary **⑪ Bourbon Steak** caters to sleek Georgetowners and a who's who of Washington who enjoy their steaks—and don't mind paying $40 to $50 for one. The elegant lounge offers views of Georgetown's C&O Canal. *2800 Pennsylvania Ave. NW. ☎ 202/944-2026. www.bourbon-steakdc.com. $$$. No Metro access.*

The tree-lined streets of Georgetown.

Penn Quarter

1. National Museum of Women in the Arts
2. Madame Tussaud's
3. Cowgirl Creamery
4. Ford's Theatre National Historic Site
5. Matchbox
6. National Building Museum
7. Marian Koshland Science Museum
8. International Spy Museum
9. Verizon Center
10. Proof
11. Shakespeare Theatre

Just 15 years ago, this section of town induced more fear than fanfare. Now Penn Quarter has certifiably transformed, drawing beautiful young things in droves to explore it. The former red-light district has been replaced with scene-making lounges and high-end hotels. And art galleries, edgy theater companies, and groovy retailers have taken over aging buildings and given them new life. Throw in the Verizon Center for major sporting events and stadium concerts, and you've got one happening neighborhood. START: **Metro to Archives/Navy Memorial**

① **National Museum of Women in the Arts.** One of the lesser-known museums in the city, but nonetheless important, the NMWA is the only one dedicated solely to showcasing women artists in the country. More than 3,000 works comprise the collection of art from women from the 16th century to the present. ⏱ *1 hr. 1250 New York Ave. NW.* ☎ *202/783-5000.*

www.nmwa.org. Metro: Metro Center.

② ★ **Madame Tussaud's.** Visit the Oval Office and meet President Barack Obama and First Lady Michelle—or at least their wax figures—at this institution that also features other important political, sports, and music figures of Washington. ⏱ *1 hr. 1001 F St. NW.*

www.madametussauds.com/
washington. Hours vary. Metro:
Gallery Place/Chinatown.

③ Cowgirl Creamery. No trip to
the area would be complete without
a quick stop at this Paris-like wine
shop. Stock up on a variety of gourmet cheeses and wine before continuing your tour of the area. 🕐 *10
min. 919 F St. NW.* ☎ *202/393-6880.
www.cowgirlcreamery.com. Metro:
Gallery Place/Chinatown.*

**④ ★★ Ford's Theatre
National Historic Site.** On April
14, 1865, gun-wielding assassin John
Wilkes Booth killed President Abraham Lincoln here, as the president
watched a performance of *Our American Cousin.* Booth crept into the president's box; shot Lincoln; leapt to the
stage, shouting, "Sic semper tyran-
nis!" ("Thus ever to tyrants!"); and
then mounted his horse in the alley
and galloped off. Doctors carried Lincoln across the street to the house of
William Petersen, where the president
died the next morning. The theater
closed immediately, and the War
Department used the building as an
office until 1893, when three floors
collapsed, killing 22 clerks. Subse-
quently, the structure fell into disuse

The International Spy Museum.

until 1968, when it reopened—
restored to its appearance on the
night of Lincoln's murder—as a functioning playhouse and a repository for
historical artifacts surrounding the
assassination and the trial of Booth's
conspirators. The collection of
museum artifacts includes Booth's
derringer pistol, Lincoln's overcoat
from the night he was shot, and the
theater binoculars that were found on
the floor of the president's box. A

The newly renovated Ford's Theatre.

2009 renovation expanded exhibits; added a new lobby and box office; and installed 21st-century lighting, seats, and concessions. ⏲ *1½ hr., or more if you plan to see a show. 511 10th St. NW.* ☎ *202/347-4833. www.fordstheatre.org. Museum admission $2.50. Limited free tickets available at 8:30am on first-come, first-served basis. Daily 8:30am–5:30pm, except Dec 25. Metro: Archive/Navy Memorial.*

Built into a 15-foot-wide (4.5m), three-story tall building, **5 Matchbox** is quite simply the place for pizza. You'll happily nosh on fire-cooked pizza pies, mini-burgers, and salads—if you can get a table. *Note:* Your entire party must be present before they'll seat you. *713 H St. NW.* ☎ *202/289-4441. www. matchboxdc.com. $$. Metro: Gallery Place/Chinatown.*

6 ★★ National Building Museum. Architects of the world, rejoice! Finally, a museum is dedicated to American achievements in the building arts. ⏲ *45 min. 401 F St. NW.* ☎ *202/272-2448. www.nbm. org. Admission $8; $5 seniors, youth, students (age 3-17). Mon–Sat 10am–5pm; Sun 11am–5pm. Metro: Gallery Place/Chinatown. See p 46.*

7 Marian Koshland Science Museum. Want to know how DNA works, or how global warming will affect us? You don't have to be a science geek to immerse yourself for hours in this museum. ⏲ *2 hr. 6th and E sts. NW.* ☎ *202/334-1201. www.koshland-science-museum.org. Admission $7 adults, $4 students. Wed–Mon 10am–6pm (last admission 5pm), except Thanksgiving, Dec 25, and Jan 1–13. Metro: Gallery Place/Chinatown.*

8 ★★ International Spy Museum. The word "spy" used to conjure up romantic images of James Bond and trench-coated secret agents. Now, in the wake of 9/11 and terrorist cells, it's a whole new world. To learn about the history of espionage and the uncharted territory we now must learn to navigate, tour this museum, which features the largest collection of international espionage artifacts ever put on public display. Exhibits include a re-creation of a tunnel beneath the divided city of Berlin during the Cold War; the intelligence-gathering stories of those behind enemy lines and of those involved in planning D-Day in World War II; an exhibit on escape and evasion techniques in wartime; the tales of more recent spies, told by the CIA and FBI agents involved in identifying them; and a mockup of an intelligence agency's 21st-century operations center. The Spy Museum's executive director was

The National Building Museum.

Al fresco dining at Proof.

with the CIA for 36 years and his advisory board includes two former CIA directors, two former CIA disguise chiefs, and a retired KGB general. ⏲ *2 hr. 800 F St. NW.* ☎ *202/393-7798. www.spymuseum. org. Metro: Gallery Place/Chinatown.*

9 Verizon Center. Time it right and you could catch a game of hoops by the Wizards, or the puckish Alex Ovechkin making goals for the Caps. You might even see Madonna or another touring legend in concert when you come here for stadium-size entertainment. ⏲ *30 min., or more if you plan to catch a game or a show. 601 F St. NW.* ☎ *202/628-3200. www.verizon center.com. Call for admission prices. Metro: Gallery Place/Chinatown.*

Wine bars exploded onto the D.C. scene in recent years, and **10 ★★★ Proof** continues to be at the top of the heap. A tax attorney-turned-restaurateur, Mark Kuller opened this wine-centric restaurant in 2007 and devoted much of his own wine collection to its list, which boasts 1,000 different bottles. A dinner of glazed Alaskan sablefish or grilled beef hanger steak isn't bad, either. *775 G St. NW.* ☎ *202/ 737-7663. www.proofdc.com. $$–$$$. Metro: Gallery Place/Chinatown.*

11 ★★ Shakespeare Theatre. From *Love's Labor Lost* to *Pericles,* this renowned outfit stages the best of the Bard in one of the District's hottest new neighborhoods. Fill up on highbrow culture, then hit the town for some low-down gallivanting after the show. ⏲ *30 min., or more if you plan to see a show. Metro: Gallery Place/Chinatown.* *See p 19.*

Capitol Hill

1. Union Station
2. Sewall-Belmont House & Museum
3. Folger Shakespeare Library
4. Bartholdi Park
5. Capitol Hill Books
6. Barracks Row
7. Ted's Bulletin
8. Eastern Market
9. Washington Navy Yard
10. Bullfeathers

Although it's the seat of U.S. government, crowned by the Capitol's graceful dome, and encompassing the Supreme Court and the Library of Congress, "the Hill" is also a quiet residential district bounded by the Capitol to the west, the Armory to the east, H Street to the north, and the Southwest Freeway to the south. With its tree-lined streets of Victorian homes, restaurants, the U.S. Botanic Garden, and the Folger Shakespeare Library, Capitol Hill offers plenty of reasons to visit beyond its government buildings. For a more extensive tour of this historic neighborhood and its essential landmarks, see "The Best of D.C. in Two Days," on p 14. Here are a few additional highlights, for a more relaxed day of exploration rather than sightseeing. START: **Metro to Eastern Market**

---

1 ★ Union Station. Take one step inside and you'll know that this is no typical train station. As ornate as it is functional, this 1907 Beaux Arts–style building was designed by noted architect Daniel Burnham. As a member of the illustrious McMillan Commission (assembled in 1900 to

beautify the city in a manner befitting an important world capital), Burnham counseled, "Make no little plans. They have no magic to stir men's blood." Union Station, one of the commission's "big plans," (at its opening it was the largest train station in the world), was modeled after the baths of Diocletian and the Arch of Constantine in Rome. The Main Hall features a nine-story, 96-foot (29m) barrel-vaulted ceiling inlaid with 70 pounds (32 kg) of 22-karat gold-leaf, acres of white marble floors punctuated by red Champlain dots, bronze grilles, and rich Honduran mahogany paneling. The adjacent East Hall has scagliola marbled walls and columns; a gorgeous, hand-stenciled skylight ceiling; and stunning murals inspired by the frescos of Pompeii. In the heyday of rail travel, many important events took place in Union Station: Visiting royalty and heads of state were honored here, as were World War I General Pershing, upon his return from France; South Pole explorer Rear Admiral Byrd; and President Franklin Delano Roosevelt, whose funeral train was met here by thousands of mourners in 1945. Today Union Station is a crossroads for D.C. locals, commuters from Baltimore and the suburbs, and visitors from farther afield. It also houses loads of shops such as Nine West, Swatch, and Victoria's Secret, plus a solid section of fast-food and fine-fare dining options. ⏰ *30 min.* 2 *Massachusetts Ave. NE.* ☎ *202/289-1908. www.unionstationdc.com. Free admission. Daily 24 hr. Metro: Union Station.*

❷ Sewall-Belmont House & Museum. You might find yourself humming "Sister Suffragette" from *Mary Poppins*—"We're clearly soldiers in petticoats, and dauntless crusaders for women's votes"—as you tour this museum. This Federal/Queen Anne–style house was once the home of Alice Paul (1885–1977), who founded the National Women's Party in 1913 and wrote the original Equal Rights Amendment to the Constitution (ERA). Paul, who held three law degrees and a Ph.D. in sociology, was jailed seven times in the U.S. and Great Britain for the cause of women's suffrage. Paul lived here from 1929 to 1972, but now the National Women's Party owns and maintains the house. Exhibitions trace the path of the women's movement, from the better-known activist Susan B. Anthony, to 59¢ buttons and the ERA. Check out picketing banners,

Inside the Sewall-Belmont House.

5,000 prints and photographs, original cartoons, more than 50 scrapbooks from early suffragists, paintings, sculptures, publications, and more. ⏲ *1 hr. 144 Constitution Ave. NE.* ☎ *202/546-1210. www. sewallbelmont.org. Admission $5. Wed–Sun noon–5pm. Metro: Union Station.*

③ ★★ **Folger Shakespeare Library.** Founded in 1932 by ardent Shakespeare fan (and wealthy Standard Oil executive) Henry Clay Folger and his wife, Emily, this repository houses the world's largest collection of the Bard's printed works. In addition to its 250,000 books—100,000 of which are classified as rare—the library also provides an important research center for students of the master playwright and Renaissance literature. The permanent exhibits in the Great Hall include period costumes, musical instruments,

historical playbills, and more. ⏲ *45 min. 201 E. Capitol St. SE.* ☎ *202/544-7077. www.folger.edu. Mon–Sat 10am–5pm; Sun noon–5pm; with docent tours at 11am and 3pm weekdays, Sat–Sun 1pm; closed on federal holidays. Metro: Capitol South or Union Station.*

④ ★★ **Bartholdi Park.** Part of the U.S. Botanic Garden, this flower-filled park is about the size of a city block and is named for the French sculptor who created its 30-foot-high (9m) cast-iron "fountain of light and water." Frederic Auguste Bartholdi (1834–1904), who is most famous for that other large sculpture he made—the Statue of Liberty in New York Harbor—constructed this work for the 1876 International Exposition in Philadelphia. When the exposition closed, the U.S. government purchased the sculpture for the National Mall; it was moved to its current location in 1932. Come to

The Folger Shakespeare Library.

A MIDSOMMER NIGHTS DREAME

Capitol Hill Books.

view it, and to enjoy the surrounding sunflowers, petunias, morning glories, tall ornamental grasses, and creeping vines. ⏱ *45 min. 1st St. and Independence Ave. SW. Free admission. Daily dawn–dusk. Metro: Union Station.*

5 ★ Capitol Hill Books. This spot is a mecca for bibliophiles and lovers of used books. Spend some time wandering this quirky book maze and you'll find some of the more unique titles in literary history. ⏱ *30 min. 657 C St. SE.* ☎ *202/544-1621. www.capitolhillbooks-dc.com. Mon–Fri 11:30am–6pm. Sat–Sun 9am–6pm. Metro: Eastern Market.*

6 ★★ Barracks Row. The strip along 8th St. SE became the first commercial center in D.C. after Thomas Jefferson centered the Marine Corps there in 1801. The neighborhood has ridden out some downturns since then, but in more recent years, Washingtonians have flocked to the lively district for housing, dining, and shopping. Restaurants, outdoor cafes, and taverns such as the Ugly Mug and Belga Café are always packed, and stores such as Groovy DC and Homebody cater to artsy types seeking those one-of-a-kind finds. ⏱ *1 hr. 8th and Eye sts. SE.* ☎ *202/544-3188. www.barracksrow.org. Metro: Eastern Market.*

Capitol Hill is known for its stuffy, only-in-D.C. restaurants, but **7 ★ Ted's Bulletin**—a lively American eatery, with close tables and a neighborly feel—is anything but. Dig into delicious salads and burgers, but save room for dessert—the milkshakes and pies are top-notch here. *505 8th St. SE.* ☎ *202/544-8337. www.tedsbulletin.com. Breakfast, lunch, dinner. $–$$. Metro: Eastern Market.*

8 ★★ Eastern Market. You'll have many "have-to-have-it" moments during your stroll through the shops of this D.C. landmark that has been in continuous operation since 1873. A 2007 fire nearly decimated the 135-year-old East Hall building, but the city government—and devoted fans of the market—vowed to rebuild it, and it reopened in June 2009. Snack on treats from various vendors to stay fueled as you browse the wares of more than 175 exhibitors who showcase their handmade pottery, jewelry, crafts, furniture, and—on the weekends—fresh produce from the surrounding

Daniel Burnham's Beaux-Arts masterwork, Union Station.

states. Saturday morning is the best time to go experience a D.C. tradition: blueberry pancakes at the Market Lunch counter (Sat 7am–6pm; Sun 9am–4pm; Tues–Fri from 7am). ⏱ *2 hr. 7th St. & N. Carolina Ave. SE. ☎ 202/543-7470. Tues–Fri 7am–7pm; Sat 7am–6pm; Sun 9am–5pm. Metro: Eastern Market.*

⑨ Washington Navy Yard. If you're already in the Capitol Hill area, it's a relatively short walk to the Washington Navy Yard and Museum. Off the beaten track and often overlooked—and thus blessedly uncrowded—this museum celebrates the Navy's heroes, ships, diplomacy, and battles. Among its many exhibits are submarines, swords, and firearms from Revolutionary ship captains, artifacts from salvaged Naval vessels dating back to 1800, and a range of Naval uniforms that span the years. ⏱ *1 hr. 805 Kidder Breese SE. ☎ 202/433-6826. www.history.navy.mil. Free admission. Mon–Fri 9am–5pm, Sat–Sun and holidays 10am–5pm. Call in advance for tour reservations. Metro: Eastern Market or Navy Yard.*

The venerable **⑩ Bullfeathers** is where everyone—Democrats, Republicans, staffers, and Hill members—goes for strong drinks when the working day is done. Eavesdrop on conversations and you might just hear some of those famous D.C. secrets. *410 1st SE. ☎ 202/543-5005. www.bullfeathersdc.com. $$. Metro: Capitol South.* ●

Bullfeathers, a Capitol Hill standby.

Shopping Best Bets

Best **Interior Design District**
★★ Cady's Alley, *3314 M St. NW, Georgetown (p 111)*

Best **Antiques (to $10K)**
Susquehanna Antique Co., *3206 O St. NW (see "Antique Row," p 112)*

Best **Antiques (to $100)**
★★ Eastern Market, *7th Street and North Carolina Avenue SE (p 114)*

Best **"Bling"**
★★★ Tiny Jewel Box, *1147 Connecticut Ave. NW (p 113)*

Best **Shoes for $500**
★★ Sassanova, *1641 Wisconsin Ave. NW. (p 114)*

Best **Shoes for $50**
Nine West, *1029 Connecticut Ave. NW (p 110)*

Best **Apparel for Serious Fashionistas**
★ Urban Chic, *1626 Wisconsin Ave. NW (p 110)*

Best **Commercial Shopping Drag**
M Street and Wisconsin Avenue

Best **Hidden Gem**
Home Rule, *187 14th St. NW (p 112)*

Best **Hood for Contemporary Art**
★★★ The Galleries on 14th Street, *14th Street NW (p 108)*

Best **Place for a Power Tie**
★★★ Thomas Pink, *1127 Connecticut Ave. NW (p 110)*

Best **Gourmet Snack**
★ Dean & Deluca, *3276 M St. NW (p 111)*

Best **Flowers**
★ Ultra Violet Flowers, *1218 31st St. NW (p 111)*

Best Bookstore to **Catch a Senator Reading about Himself**
★ Capitol Hill Books, *657 C St. SE (p 108)*

Best for Cool **Mid-20th-Century Finds**
Miss Pixie's, *1626 14th St. NW (p 112)*

Best **Baby Stuff**
★★ Dawn Price Baby, *3112 M St., NW (p 108)*

Best for **Contemporary Home Design**
★★ Muléh, *1831 14th St. NW (p 112)*

Best **Denim**
★★ Denim Bar, *1109 S. Joyce St., Arlington, Va. (p 109)*

Best **Cards & Gifts**
★ Pulp DC, *1803 14th St. NW (p 110)*

Best for **Musicians**
Middle C Music, *4530 Wisconsin Ave. NW (p 113)*

Best **Bones to Pick**
★★ Metro Mutts, *508 H St. NE (p 113)*

Best for **Innovative Children's Toys**
Tugooh Toys, *1419 Wisconsin Ave. NW (p 108)*

Previous page: Antiques and home furnishings at Miss Pixie's (p 112).

Capitol Hill & Penn Quarter

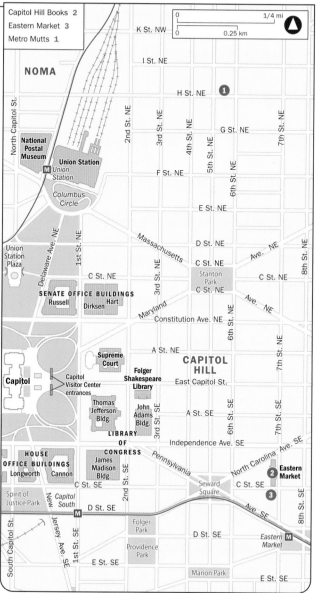

Capitol Hill Books **2**
Eastern Market **3**
Metro Mutts **1**

NOMA

K St. NW

I St. NE

H St. NE **1**

National
Postal
Museum

Ⓜ Union Station

Union
Station

Columbus
Circle

2nd St. NE

3rd St. NE

4th St. NE

5th St. NE

G St. NE

6th St. NE

7th St. NE

F St. NE

E St. NE

North Capitol St.

Union
Station
Plaza

Delaware Ave. NE

1st St. NE

Massachusetts

D St. NE

Ave. NE

8th St. NE

C St. NE

C St. NE

Stanton
Park

C St. NE

C St. NE

3rd St. NE

Maryland

SENATE OFFICE BUILDINGS
Russell   Dirksen Hart

Constitution Ave. NE

6th St. NE

Ave. NE

A St. NE

7th St. NE

Supreme
Court

Capitol

Capitol
Visitor Center
entrances

Folger
Shakespeare
Library

CAPITOL
HILL

East Capitol St.

Thomas
Jefferson
Bldg.

John
Adams
Bldg.

3rd St. SE

A St. SE

6th St. SE

7th St. SE

LIBRARY
OF
CONGRESS

Independence Ave. SE

HOUSE
OFFICE BUILDINGS
Longworth   Cannon

James
Madison
Bldg.

Pennsylvania

North Carolina Ave. SE

2 Eastern
Market

C St. SE

Spirit of
Justice Park

New Jersey Ave. SE

Capitol
South

2nd St. SE

C St. SE

Seward
Square

3

Ave. SE

8th St. SE

Ⓜ

D St. SE

Folger
Park

D St. SE

Eastern **Ⓜ**
Market

South Capitol St.

1st St. SE

E St. SE

Providence
Park

Marion Park

E St. SE

Georgetown & Dupont Circle

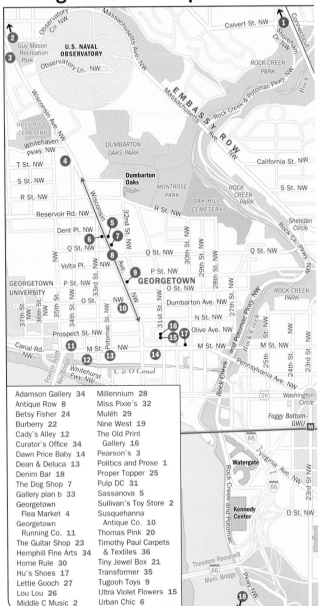

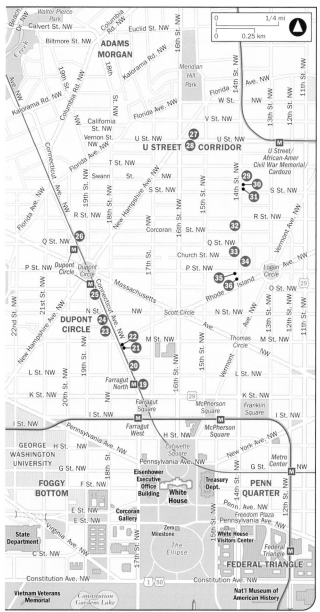

Shopping A to Z

Art

★★★ The Galleries on 14th Street
14TH STREET/LOGAN CIRCLE   The creative mark made on 14th Street has inspired curators to open galleries on this emerging main street for modern and contemporary works. Don't miss these highlights: **Hemphill Fine Arts** (☎ 202/234-5601; www.hemphill finearts.com; AE, DC, DISC, MC, V); **Adamson Gallery** (☎ 202/232-0707; www.adamsoneditions.com; MC, V); **Curator's Office** (☎ 202/387-1008; www.curatorsoffice.com; MC, V); **Transformer** (1404 P St. NW at 14th St.; ☎ 202/483-1102; www.transformerdc.org); and **Gallery plan b** (1530 14th St. NW at Q St.; ☎ 202/234-2711; www.gallery planb.com; AE, MC, V). Metro: Cardozo/U St. Map p 106.

Babies & Kids

★★ Dawn Price Baby
GEORGETOWN   If you're a member of the stroller set whose bundle of joy must have the latest Bugaboo model, head to this small but stocked shop. Clothing, shoes, and toys are also for sale. 3112 M St. NW (at 31st St.). ☎ 202/333-3939. www.dawnpricebaby.com. AE, DC, DISC, MC, V. No Metro access. See "Traveling to Georgetown," on p 91. Map p 106.

★ Sullivan's Toy Store
CLEVELAND PARK   Forgot to pack Elmo? This tantrum-quashing shop is jam-packed with every conceivable plaything, puzzle, costume, wheeled wonder, art supply, and entertaining distraction imaginable. 4200 Van Ness St. NW. ☎ 202/362-1343. AE, DISC, MC, V. Metro: Tenleytown. Map p 106.

Tugooh Toys
GEORGETOWN   If you're picky about toys, then head to this thoughtful shop, which is well stocked with an array of all-natural and eco-friendly toys, games, books, and clothes. 1419 Wisconsin Ave. NW. ☎ 202/333-0032. AE, DISC, MC, V. No Metro Access. See "Traveling to Georgetown," on p 91. Map p 106.

Books

★ Capitol Hill Books
CAPITOL HILL   Feel like losing yourself on a rainy afternoon in dusty stacks bursting with amazing old books? This used bookstore, steps from Eastern Market, has more than a century's worth of history and is a mine for modern first editions, lit-crit, and unusual subjects. 657 C St. SE (btw. 6th and 7th sts.). ☎ 202/544-1621. www.capitolhillbooks-dc.com. AE, DC, MC, V. Metro: Eastern Market. Map p 105.

★★ Politics and Prose
CLEVELAND PARK   If on principle you'd rather give your hard-earned cash to Mom and Pop than a big chain, head north of downtown to this two-story shop. It's famed in D.C. for its warm vibe, nearly nightly author readings, excellent selection, and cozy coffeehouse. 5015 Connecticut Ave. NW (at Fessenden St.). ☎ 202/364-1919. www.politics-prose.com. AE, DISC, MC, V. Metro: Van Ness–UDC, then walk or transfer to an "L" bus for 1 mile (1.6km). Map p 106.

Fashion

★ Betsy Fisher
DUPONT CIRCLE   You follow Vogue, so peruse the racks of this boutique—buzz to gain entry, please—designed to suit the caviar tastes of well-dressed women who must look smashing at D.C. dinner parties and occasional dates with high-ranking officials. 1224

Capitol Hill Books.

Connecticut Ave. NW (at 18th St.).
☎ *202/785-1975. www.betsyfisher.com. AE, DISC, MC, V. Metro: Dupont Circle. Map p 106.*

★★ **Burberry** DOWNTOWN Yes, it's a chain store. But despite its English roots, there is something about that famous signature plaid—found in the linings of its cloth umbrellas, tony and tailored clothing, and camel-hair coats for men and women—that is quintessentially Washington, too. *1155 Connecticut Ave. NW (at M St.).* ☎ *202/463-3000. www.burberry.com. AE, DISC, MC, V. Metro: Farragut North. Map p 106.*

★★ **Denim Bar** BETHESDA We wouldn't send a D.C. newcomer to shop outside the District for anything but the ultimate pair of jeans. Men and women devoted to upscale designer denim should take the easy Metro ride here, where an expert staff will guide you (sometimes cruelly, to be kindly) to the perfect fit. *1101 S. Joyce St., Arlington, Virginia.* ☎ *703/414-8202. www.denimbaronline.com. AE, DISC, MC, V. Metro: Pentagon City. Map p 106.*

Georgetown Running Co.
GEORGETOWN If you're light on your feet—meaning the prospect of running 5 miles (8km) fills you with joy, not dread—jog this way for state-of-the-art track shoes and gear. *3401 M St. NW (at 34th St.).* ☎ *202/337-8626. www.therunningcompany.net. AE, DISC, MC, V. No Metro access. See "Traveling to Georgetown," on p 91. Map p 106.*

Lettie Gooch SHAW A little bit of NYC's Soho is found in this unique boutique that stocks one-of-a-kind feminine fashions from Tricia Fix, SaltWorks, Hype, Jak & Rae, and local designers. *1517 U St. NW.* ☎ *202/332-4242. www.lettiegooch.com. Metro: U Street/Cardozo. Map p 106.*

Lou Lou DUPONT CIRCLE Head to this boutique for any accessory you could ever want, from beaded necklaces to brooches to headbands to handbags—all at very reasonable prices. *1601 Connecticut*

Friendship Heights, D.C.

Known and loved for its off-the-beaten-path boutiques and shops, this bustling strip is billed as D.C.'s Fifth Avenue. If it's the extremely high-end you're looking for, take a 15-minute Metro ride—or better yet, hail a cab—to this busy Wisconsin Avenue corridor that caters to luxury buyers with outposts of Sak's Fifth Avenue, Tiffany's, Louis Vuitton, Jimmy Choo, Neiman Marcus, Bloomingdales, and more. Be prepared to drop some serious Benjamins on designer dresses, impeccable suits, handbags, and jewelry in this pricey neighborhood along the Maryland border. *Wisconsin and Western aves. Metro: Friendship Heights.*

Proper Topper.

Ave. NW. Nearby locations in Georgetown, Penn Quarter, and Bethesda. ☎ 202/588-0027. www. loulouboutiques.com. AE, MC, V. Metro: Dupont Circle. Map p 106.

Nine West DOWNTOWN Already well-known from coast to coast, this stand-alone outpost carries inexpensive boots, espadrilles, and flats to have you stepping pretty in the city. 1029 Connecticut Ave. NW. ☎ 202/331-3243. www.ninewest.com. Metro: Farragut North. Map p 106.

Proper Topper DUPONT CIRCLE From the name alone, you can probably guess what this tiny shop specializes in. Every type of hat, cap, and beret in stylish designs is represented, along with picture frames, gift books, and funky clothes. 1350 Connecticut Ave. NW. ☎ 202/842-3055. www.propertopper.com. Metro: Dupont Circle. Map p 106.

★★★ **Thomas Pink** DOWNTOWN Dapper gentlemen from the nation's capital descend upon this London outpost for well-cut business suits, power ties, cufflinks, crisp and colorful shirts, and tailored service. Inside the Mayflower Hotel. 1127 Connecticut Ave. NW (btw. L and M sts.). ☎ 202/223-5390. www.thomas pink.com. AE, MC, V. Metro: Farragut North. Map p 106.

★ **Urban Chic** GEORGETOWN If you dress like a casual-but-chic Hollywood starlet, and you're intent on finding chandelier earrings, a slouched hobo bag, a flirty blouse, or pricey designer denim, then off you go: Urban Chic awaits. 1626 Wisconsin Ave. NW (btw. Q St. and Reservoir Rd.). ☎ 202/338-5398. www. urbanchic-dc.com. AE, DISC, MC, V. No Metro access. See "Traveling to Georgetown," on p 91. Map p 106.

Flowers & Gifts
★ **Pulp DC** 14TH STREET A former San Francisco AIDS activist opened this community-welcoming gift shop in 2001. People can sit at the "card

Pulp DC.

Housewares at Cady's Alley in Georgetown.

bar" to journal; write notes on unusual, handcrafted cards; or chat with neighbors. *1803 14th St. NW (at S St.).* ☎ *202/462-7857. www.pulpdc. com. AE, DISC, MC, V. Metro: Cardozo/U St. Map p 106.*

★ **Ultra Violet Flowers** GEORGE-TOWN   In the doghouse? Wooing your beloved? Mother's Day? No matter. Call Ultra Violet for a floral concoction exploding with color and sweet, intoxicating scents. *1218 31st St. NW (near M St.).* ☎ *202/ 333-3002. www.ultravioletflowersdc. com. AE, MC, V. No Metro access. See "Traveling to Georgetown," on p 91. Map p 106.*

Food & Wine
★ **Dean & Deluca** GEORGETOWN Crave a dark chocolate bar from Switzerland? How about a custard fruit tart? Gourmands with a nose for fragrant cheeses, fresh fish, out-of-season fruit, choice-cut meats, aged wines, Kona coffee beans, and European crackers shop and nosh here. In fine weather, enjoy lunch at the outdoor cafe. *3276 M St. NW (at Potomac St.).* ☎ *202/342-2500. www.deandeluca.com. AE, DISC, MC, V. No Metro access. See "Traveling to Georgetown," on p 91. Map p 106.*

★ **Pearson's** GLOVER PARK   This neighborhood standby sells more than 2,000 fine wines, liqueurs, and spirits. A knowledgeable staff of 15

experts hosts regular wine tastings. *2436 Wisconsin Ave. NW (at 37th St.).* ☎ *202/333-6666. www.pearsons wine.com. MC, V. Bus line: D1 or D2. Map p 106.*

Furniture & Home Design
Antique Row GEORGETOWN Depending on which way you're walking, Antique Row is either a cool cruise downhill or a steep trek up it. In any event, antiques lovers won't care—they'll be too busy gaping at the storefronts with mint-condition 18th-century divans, beautifully painted Persian consoles, weathered ceramic water jugs, and other singular finds. The best of the lot: Carling Nichols; Gore-Dean; and, for early-20th-century fans, Random Harvest. Bring your black Amex card for this shopping stroll—prices are steep. *Wisconsin Ave., from S St. to N St. No Metro access. See "Traveling to Georgetown," on p 91. Map p 106.*

★★ **Cady's Alley** GEORGETOWN Make tracks to Washington's newest district devoted to furnishings and accessories. Not long ago, Cady's Alley was all industrial space and abandoned lofts. Now, if you walk through a bricked archway off M Street and descend a flight of stairs into a hidden alcove, you'll discover shops such as Contemporaria for Italian furniture, Bulthaup for ultraluxe culinary gadgets, Illuminations

Home Rule.

for European lighting, and Poggen-pohl Studio for German kitchen fixtures. *3300 block of M St. NW. www.cadysalley.com. No Metro access. See "Traveling to Georgetown," on p 91. Map p 106.*

Home Rule U STREET Funky furnishings, housewares, kitchen gadgets, and bath items are packed into this storefront. Have a kid who likes to cook? You'll find great gifts of all variety here. *1807 14th St. NW. 202/797-5544. www.homerule.com. Metro: U Street/Cardozo. Map p 106.*

★★ Millennium U STREET/CARDOZO Do you groove on pleather chairs, mid-20th-century coffee tables, stainless steel bookcases, or even white vinyl microminis? Millennium is a must for fans of design from the '50s, '60s, and '70s. *1528 U St. NW (at 15th St.). 202/483-1218. Metro: Cardozo/U St. Map p 106.*

Miss Pixie's U STREET Scavenger hunters will love Miss Pixie's giant new space, which is filled with secondhand furnishings, funky chandeliers, table settings, figurines, and other zany knickknacks (plastic flamingos, anyone?). *1626 14th St. NW. 202/232-8171. www.misspixies.com. Metro: U Street/Cardozo. Map p 106.*

★★ Muléh 14TH STREET Owner Christopher Reiter mixes it up at Muléh (pronounced "moo-lay") with his Asian-inspired collection of wooden benches and tables, minimalist bed frames, sophisticated bric-a-brac, and racks of city-slick clothing by young designers. *1831 14th St. NW (at Swann St.). 202/667-3440. www.muleh.com. AE, MC, V. Metro: Cardozo/U St. Map p 106.*

The Old Print Gallery GEORGETOWN Fans of old prints and maps from the 16th century and up will revel in this tiny shop's collection that features only originals—no reproductions—and many with scenes of D.C. *1220 31st St. N. 202/965-1818. www.oldprintgallery.com. No Metro access. See "Traveling to Georgetown," on p 91. Map p 106.*

Susquehanna Antique Company GEORGETOWN Peruse a wide selection of 17th-, 18th- and 19th-century antiques and fine art, plus unique cast-iron decorations, at this antiques company in Georgetown. *3216 O St. NW (btw. Wisconsin Ave. and Potomac St.). 202/333-1511. www.susquehannaantiques.com. No Metro access. See "Traveling to Georgetown," on p 91. Map p 106.*

Muléh.

Browse clothing and accessories at Muléh.

Timothy Paul Carpets & Textiles LOGAN CIRCLE
Interior design enthusiasts, make a mental note to visit this husband-and-wife-owned boutique/gallery, specializing in custom-colored textiles, upscale carpet lines, antique rugs, and unusual lighting fixtures. *1404 14th St. NW (at Rhode Island Ave.).* ☎ *202/319-1100. www.timothypaulcarpets.com. AE, MC, V. Metro: McPherson Sq. or Dupont Circle. Map p 106.*

Jewelry
★★★ **Tiny Jewel Box** DOWNTOWN   Thinking of popping the question or surprising your sweetie with a fabulous bauble, expensive watch, or eye-popping ring from an estate sale? Look no further than this D.C. mainstay, a peddler of romantic, unique adornments. *1147 Connecticut Ave. NW (at M St.).* ☎ *202/393-2747. www.tinyjewel box.com. AE, MC, V. Metro: Farragut North. Map p 106.*

Music & Musical Instruments
★ **The Guitar Shop** DUPONT CIRCLE   Aspiring Cobains, Springs-teens, and Youngs converge here to pluck strings, caress Fenders and Rickenbackers, and brag about their next (or last) gigs to the authentic (if occasionally bitter) musicians behind the cash registers. *1216 Connecticut Ave. NW (at Jefferson St.).* ☎ *202/331-7333. www.theguitar shop.com. DISC, MC, V. Metro: Dupont Circle. Map p 106.*

Middle C Music TENLEYTOWN
Looking for the perfect drum set or sheet music for the aspiring musician? Stop in to this packed shop that carries music of all genres, accessories, gifts, books—and hosts lessons, too. *4530 Wisconsin Ave. NW.* ☎ *202/244-7326. www. middlecmusic.com. DISC, MC, V. Metro: Tenleytown. Map p 106.*

Pets
The Dog Shop GEORGETOWN
Fido gets the star treatment here,

Timothy Paul Carpet & Textiles.

Tiny Jewel Box.

where you can grab gourmet treats, supplies, and toys. A huge plus: They deliver. *1625 Wisconsin Ave. NW. ☎ 202/337-3647. www.dog shopdc.com. No Metro access. See "Traveling to Georgetown," on p 91. Map p 106.*

★★ Metro Mutts H STREET
Spoiled felines and diva dogs know where to send their masters for all-organic kibble; irresistible catnip; pigs' ears; and designer bones, collars, harnesses, and other supplies. *508 H St. NE. ☎ 202/450-5661. www. metromuttsdc.com. AE, DISC, MC, V. Metro: Union Station. Map p 105.*

Shoes
★★ Hu's Shoes GEORGETOWN
A rather daunting showroom—you might be the only customer fending off several hungry salespeople—displays the latest and greatest in women's "rebellious" designer shoes, including Sonia Rykiel, Chloé, Proenza Schouler, and more. *3005 M St. NW (at 30th St.). ☎ 202/342-0202. www.hushoes.com. AE, DC, DISC, MC, V. No Metro access. See "Traveling to Georgetown," on p 91. Map p 106.*

★★ Sassanova GEORGETOWN
"Stylish women in Washington" ceased to be an oxymoron when Sassanova opened up in 2004, carrying designers such as Bettye Muller, Lambertson Truex, Holly-would, and Lulu Guinness, in sweet slingbacks, saucy stilettos, wicked wedges, and funky flats. ***Warning:*** Expect to blow at least $200 here. *1641 Wisconsin Ave. NW (at 33rd St.). ☎ 202/471-4400. www. sassanova.com. AE, MC, V. No Metro access. See "Traveling to Georgetown," on p 91. Map p 106.*

Thrift & Flea Markets
★★ Eastern Market CAPITOL HILL If Washingtonians could name only one institution endemic to the city that had nothing to do with politics, 9 out of 10 would say Eastern Market. Locals gather here on weekends for the flea market, outdoor vendors, artisans, and brunch spots. Its permanent buildings are open year-round, Tuesday through Sunday; the outdoor lot fills on weekends (Mar–Dec) with farmers and fresh produce, plus bargain hunters looking to score great deals. *225 7th St. SE (btw. N. Carolina Ave. and C St. SE). ☎ 202/698-5253. www.eastern market-dc.com. Metro: Eastern Market. Map p 105.*

Georgetown Flea Market
GEORGETOWN Every Sunday (unless it's pouring rain or freezing cold outside), bargain hunters troll the lot at the Corcoran School for cheap treasures. Score handmade and antique jewelry, velvet Elvis paintings, secondhand leather jackets, and used furniture from weathered vendors, smoking cigarettes and ready to haggle. *Wisconsin Ave. NW (at Whitehaven St. NW). www. georgetownfleamarket.com. No Metro access. See "Traveling to Georgetown," on p 91. Map p 106.* ●

6 The Best **Outdoor Activities**

The Best Outdoor Activities

Rock Creek Park

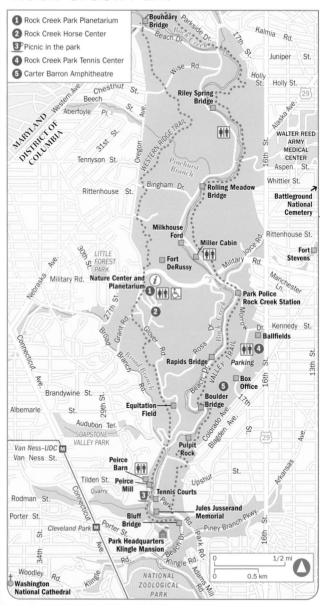

1. Rock Creek Park Planetarium
2. Rock Creek Horse Center
3. Picnic in the park
4. Rock Creek Park Tennis Center
5. Carter Barron Amphitheatre

Boundary Bridge
Parkside Dr.
Rock Creek
Beach Dr.
Kalmia Rd.
17th St.
Juniper St.
Wise Rd.
Holly St.
Holly St.
29
Chestnut St.
Beech
Aberfoyle Pl.
Western Ave.
Riley Spring Bridge
Alaska Ave.
WALTER REED ARMY MEDICAL CENTER
Aspen St.
MARYLAND
DISTRICT OF COLUMBIA
31st St.
Oregon Ave.
WESTERN RIDGE TRAIL
Pinehurst Branch
16th St.
Whittier St.
Tennyson St.
Battleground National Cemetery
Rittenhouse St.
Bingham Dr.
Rolling Meadow Bridge
Rittenhouse St.
Milkhouse Ford
Miller Cabin
Military
Joyce Rd.
Fort Stevens
30th St.
LITTLE FOREST PARK
Fort DeRussy
Manchester Ln.
Nebraska Ave.
Military Rd.
Nature Center and Planetarium
1
2
27th St.
Grant Rd.
Glover Rd.
Ross
Dr.
Rock Creek
Morrow Dr.
Park Police Rock Creek Station
Kennedy St.
Broad
Branch
Broad Branch Rd.
29th St.
Rapids Bridge
Beach Dr.
VALLEY TRAIL
Parking
Ballfields
13th St.
4
Brandywine St.
Albemarle St.
Box Office
5
Boulder Bridge
16th St.
17th St.
Connecticut Ave.
Audubon Ter.
SOAPSTONE VALLEY PARK
Equitation Field
Colorado Ave.
Blagden Ave.
29
Arkansas Ave.
Van Ness–UDC M
Van Ness St.
Pulpit Rock
Rodman St.
Peirce Barn
Tilden St.
Peirce Mill
Quarry
Upshur St.
Porter St.
Tennis Courts
3
Cleveland Park M
34th St.
Bluff Bridge
Jules Jusserand Memorial
Piney Branch Pkwy.
16th St.
Park Rd.
Woodley Rd.
Porter St.
Klingle
Rd.
Park Headquarters Klingle Mansion
Beach Dr.
Klingle Rd.
Adams Mill Rd.
Washington National Cathedral
NATIONAL ZOOLOGICAL PARK

| 0 | | 1/2 mi |
| 0 | 0.5 km | |

Previous page: Biking along the Potomac River.

How many other major American urban areas have 3,000 acres (1,214 hectares) of natural woodlands smack dab in the middle of the city? Established in 1890 by the Rock Creek Park Historic District and protected by the U.S. Congress, this green resource is to Washingtonians what Central Park is to New Yorkers—except New Yorkers can't camp, canoe, or lose themselves for miles on trails that wind beneath canopies of lush-leaved trees, so thick in spots that civilization seems a distant memory. Accessible through numerous entrance points throughout northwest Washington, this urban oasis offers shade and cooler temperatures on hot days, historic parks, great golf, horseback riding, bird-watching, a refuge for deer and raccoons, and even a 1-mile (1.6km) stretch of rapids. It also borders the National Zoo. It does have isolated areas, however, so avoid visiting early in the morning or past dusk. Be alert, and bring a friend if you can. START: **Metro to Friendship Heights or Fort Trotten, then the no. E2 bus to Glover (also called Oregon) and Military roads; walk 300 feet (91m) south on the trail to the planetarium**

Tip

Take a **virtual tour** of Rock Creek Park and explore its activities and offerings at www.nps.gov/rocr. The park runs along Rock Creek and its tributaries from the National Zoo to the D.C. boundary.

❶ ★ kids Rock Creek Park Planetarium and Nature Center. Stargazers come to the planetarium to stare at the heavens. Track the night skies here with the whole family, and take your little ones (ages 4 and up, please) to special astronomical programs on the weekends. The Nature Center is also the setting of numerous activities, including nature films, crafts demonstrations, live animal demonstrations, guided nature walks, and a daily mix of lectures and other events. Self-guided nature trails begin here. All activities are free, but you need to pick up tickets a half-hour in advance for planetarium shows. There are also nature exhibits on the premises. For a schedule, check out www.nps.gov/rocr/plan yourvisit/naturecenter.htm.

Not far from the Nature Center is **Fort DeRussy,** one of 68 fortifications erected to defend the city of Washington during the U.S. Civil War. From the intersection of Military Road and Oregon Avenue, walk a short trail through the woods to reach the fort, the remains of which include high earth mounds with openings where guns were mounted, surrounded by a deep ditch/moat. ⏱ *2 hr. Metro: See Start, above.*

Rock Creek Park is a natural haven from the bustle of the city.

② ★★ **kids** **Rock Creek Horse Center.** Next door to the planetarium, beginners can take private lessons in the ring, and more experienced riders can sign up for trail rides on weekdays with a professional trail guide. Supervised pony rides for very young children are also quite popular; there is no age limit, but your tyke must be at least 30 inches (.76m) tall to join in the fun. ⏱ *1 hr. 5100 Glover Rd.* ☎ *202/362-0117. www.rockcreekhorsecenter.com. Mon–Fri 10am–6pm.*

Once you enter wooded Rock Creek Park, you won't stumble upon too many fast-food joints in the underbrush. Bring along a lunch for a **③** 🍵 **picnic in the park** and stop at any of the 30 picnic areas throughout the grounds; some have rain shelters. Many can be reserved for groups up to 100. *Reservations for large parties must be made in person at the D.C. Department of Parks and Recreation, 3149 16th St. NW.* ☎ *202/673-7646.*

Horseback riding in Rock Creek Park.

Joggers and cyclists in Rock Creek Park.

④ **Rock Creek Park Tennis Center.** The home of the annual Legg Mason Tennis Classic offers excellent hard and soft court facilities, a pro shop, and a stadium. Free tennis courts can be found throughout the District, so if you love a good match and aren't too particular about the state of the facilities—expect faded hard courts, piles of leaves in the corners, and somewhat sagging nets—hurry to public parks such as **Montrose** (R St., btw. 30th and 31st sts.), **Rose** (P and 28th sts.), and **Volta** (34th and Volta sts.) in Georgetown, and wait your turn. (Courtesy allows for players to use the courts for 1 hour before relinquishing them to those waiting on the sidelines.) That said, those for whom well-kept facilities are a priority will enjoy the Rock Creek Park Tennis Center. ⏱ *1 hr. 16th and Kennedy sts. NW. Reservations:* ☎ *202/722-5949. www.rockcreektennis.com. Court rentals per hour $10–$19. Hours vary depending on the month.*

⑤ ★★★ **Carter Barron Amphitheatre.** Want to see Shakespeare under the stars, or catch a symphony concert or dance performance? This amphitheater, in Rock Creek Park on Colorado Avenue off 17th Street, seats 1,500 patrons. It

Theodore Roosevelt Island Park

A serene, 91-acre wilderness preserve, ★★ **Roosevelt Island Park** is a memorial to the nation's 26th president and his contributions to conservation. The swamp, marsh, and upland forest comprise a haven for rabbits, chipmunks, great owls, foxes, muskrats, turtles, and groundhogs. You can observe these flora and fauna in their natural environs on 2.5 miles (4km) of foot trails. By car, take the George Washington Memorial Parkway exit north from the Theodore Roosevelt Bridge. Parking is accessible only from the northbound lane; a pedestrian bridge connects the lot to the island. You can also rent a canoe at Thompson's Boat Center (☎ **202/333-9543;** www. thompsonboatcenter.com) and paddle over. ⏱ *3 hr. including commute.* ☎ *703/289-2500. www.nps.gov/this. Free admission. Daily dawn–dusk. Metro: Rosslyn, then walk 2 blocks to Rosslyn Circle and cross the bridge.*

opened in 1950 to commemorate the 150th anniversary of Washington as the nation's capital city. Nearly 60 years later, it's a local favorite among nature lovers and theater fans.

Some shows are free but require tickets, distributed on the day of performance at the Carter Barron Box Office (noon–8pm), and at the Washington Post building, 1150 15th St. NW (8:30am on weekdays).

Shows with admission fees are $25 at the Carter Barron Box Office, or through Ticketmaster outlets (www. ticketmaster.com). **Note:** All sales are final, even if the show is canceled; in this unlucky case, customers forfeit their tickets. ⏱ *2 hr. Bus: S1, 2, or 3. Take 16th St. N, and get off at Colorado Ave. The tennis center is a few blocks north, visible from 16th St., at Kennedy St.*

Theodore Roosevelt Island Park.

C&O Canal

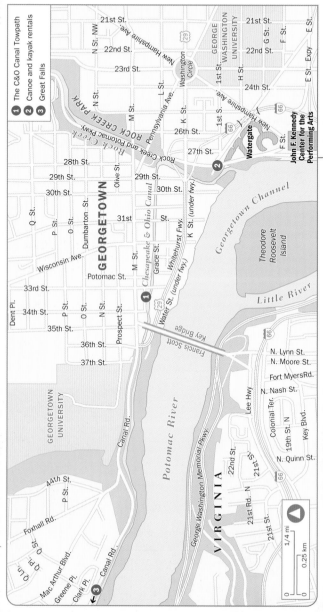

1 The C&O Canal Towpath
2 Canoe and kayak rentals
3 Great Falls

21st St.

N. St. NW

22nd St.

New Hampshire Ave.

23rd St.

Washington Circle

GEORGE WASHINGTON UNIVERSITY

21st St.

G St.

F St.

E St.

22nd St.

24th St.

E St. Expy

1st St.

H St.

New Hampshire Ave.

66

N St.

L St.

K St.

ROCK CREEK PARK

Rock Creek and Potomac Pkwy.

Pennsylvania Ave.

M St.

26th St.

F St.

John F. Kennedy Center for the Performing Arts

27th St.

2 Watergate

66

28th St.

Olive St.

29th St.

29th St.

30th St.

Georgetown Channel

29th St.

30th St.

31st

St.

Theodore Roosevelt Island

30th St.

GEORGETOWN

Q St.

P St.

O St.

Dumbarton St.

31st

K St. (under fwy.)

Whitehurst Fwy.

Wisconsin Ave.

Potomac St.

M St.

Grace St.

Chesapeake & Ohio Canal

Little River

33rd St.

34th St.

P St.

O St.

N St.

Prospect St.

1

Water St. (under fwy.)

29

Dent Pl.

35th St.

36th St.

Francis Scott Key Bridge

37th St.

N. Lynn St.

N. Moore St.

66

Fort Myers Rd.

GEORGETOWN UNIVERSITY

N. Nash St.

Potomac River

Lee Hwy

Colonial Ter.

19th St. N

Key Blvd.

Canal Rd.

N. Quinn St.

44th St.

P St.

VIRGINIA

George Washington Memorial Pkwy.

22nd St.

21st St.

21st Rd. N

Foxhall Rd.

Q Pl.

O Pl.

Greene Pl.

Mac Arthur Blvd.

Clark Pl.

Canal Rd.

3

1/4 mi

0.25 km

0

This towpath, along the Chesapeake and Ohio (C&O) Canal, is another stunning natural escape from the bustle of the city. A stretch of tree-lined land curves along the Potomac River at the canal's start in Georgetown, then winds north along the border of West Virginia before ending in Cumberland, Maryland. First opened in 1828 for the purpose of hauling coal between these two ports, the 185-mile (298km) canal and its path are now peopled with leisure boaters, joggers, bikers, power walkers, lovers out for afternoon strolls, campers, and kids. The stunning Potomac River Valley serves as an ever-changing backdrop to all this outdoor activity; summers are gorgeously green, autumn is ablaze in color, and the river itself can be placid or turbulent, but it always makes for prime viewing. START: **The Potomac River, at M or K street in Georgetown; no Metro access**

---

❶ ★ The C&O Canal Towpath. During milder months, when tourists take over the Mall, you'll find Washingtonians biking, jogging, or walking here en masse, unwinding after a long week. Start in Georgetown at the western end of K Street (beneath the Whitehurst Fwy.), and then make your way west, following the river. The first few miles are inundated with walkers, so bikers might want to take the parallel Capital Crescent Trail, which is paved and closer to the river. The Capital Crescent Trail eventually intersects with the Rock Creek Trail; take the latter for a convenient circular trip

of about 22 miles (35km). This trail and the C&O towpath meet near the 3-mile (5km) marker; track your progress with regular mile markers along the route. To rent a bike nearby, visit either of two pro shops on M Street, **Revolution Cycles** (3411 M St. NW; ☎ 202/965-3601) or **Bicycle Pro Shop** (3403 M St. NW; ☎ 202/337-0311). Or stop by **Thompson's Boat Center** (at the start of the trail in Georgetown at 2900 Virginia Ave. NW; ☎ 202/333-9543; www.thompsonboatcenter.com), which rents bicycles in addition to canoes and other river craft. ⏱ *3 hr.*

A barge on the C&O Canal.

Great Falls.

bicycle. Both outfits rent kayaks and canoes (Thompson's even offers instructional programs), and Fletcher's has a snack bar and nearby picnic grounds, too. ⏱ *2 hr.*

❸ ★★★ **Explore Great Falls.** A day trip worth taking, this 800-acre (324-hectare) park is known for its scenic beauty, steep gorges, and dramatic waterfalls and rapids, with several overlooks along the river that may take your breath away. It's along the C&O Canal, 14 miles (23km) upriver from Washington in McLean, Virginia, but ambitious bikers can reach it via the towpath. In the summer, take your family for a ride on a mule-drawn canal boat. Park rangers don period costumes as they operate replica canal boats and share the history of the canal during these trips from Great Falls. *Note:* Ten or more people are required to make a reservation. Otherwise, seats are available at a first come, first-served basis. ⏱ *3 hr. Georgetown and Great Falls barge rides: $8 per visitor (ages 15–61), $6 for seniors (ages 62 and up), $5 for children (ages 4–14), children age 3 and under ride free. Call Great Falls*

❷ **Rent a canoe or kayak.** There are two convenient boat rental centers near the start of the towpath: the aforementioned **Thompson's Boat Center** (2900 Virginia Ave. NW; ☎ 202/333-9543), and **Fletcher's Boathouse** (4940 Canal Rd. NW; ☎ 202/244-0461) at the 3-mile (5km) marker, which is easiest to reach on foot or by

Snacks & Facts

C&O Canal Visitors' Centers are scattered along the route, but only two will likely interest travelers to Washington. The first is in Georgetown (1057 Thomas Jefferson St. NW; ☎ **202/653-5190**), near the start of the towpath. It offers historical information and a quick place for a bathroom break. Hungry explorers will find no shortage of food options nearby, on K Street, Washington Harbour, and nearby M Street. The second center is **Great Falls Tavern** (11710 MacArthur Blvd., Potomac, Md.; ☎ **301/767-3714**), which provides information, restrooms, and a small snack bar. If you make it to Great Falls, consider stopping at **Old Anglers Inn** (10801 MacArthur Blvd., Potomac, MD; ☎ **301/299-9097;** entrees $29–$39; AE, DC, MC, V; lunch Tues–Sat; dinner daily; brunch Sat–Sun), for great New American fare and a fireplace.

Wheels on the Go

Washingtonians know that the Metro and taxis aren't always reliable. For a go-anywhere, do-anything mode of transport in the city, turn to Capital Bikeshare, which has quickly become one of the most popular ways to get around D.C. Sign up for a 24-hour, 3-day, 30-day, or year-long membership, and you'll have more than 1,200 bicycles at your disposal at 140 stations across the city, Virginia, and Maryland. Hop on in one location and return your bike at your destination, no back-tracking required. *Membership fees $7 (24 hrs) to $75 (annual). For more information, visit www.capital bikeshare.com.*

to confirm boats are running. From D.C. by car: Take Constitution Ave. NW/U.S. 50 to I-66 W./U.S. 50 W. out of the city across Roosevelt Memorial Bridge. Continue until you reach the U.S. 50 W./Arlington Blvd./GW Pkwy. exit. Turn north onto George Washington Memorial Pkwy. (GWMP or GW Pkwy.). Follow the GWMP to the exit for I-495 S. When you are on the ramp, stay in the right-hand lane, which will turn into the exit ramp for Rte. 193, Georgetown Pike. Take a left at the traffic light onto Rte. 193 West. In 3 miles (5 km), make a right at Old Dominion Dr. to access the park.

Hanging out in Georgetown Park, along the C&O Canal.

Georgetown

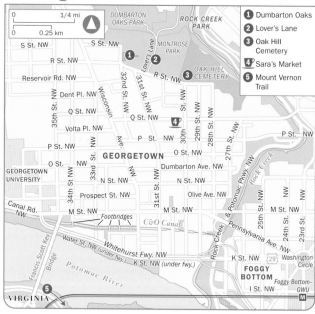

1 Dumbarton Oaks
2 Lover's Lane
3 Oak Hill Cemetery
4 Sara's Market
5 Mount Vernon Trail

The capital's most exclusive neighborhood—with its prize-winning gardens, gargantuan homes, and boldface names out walking their dogs—offers visitors an ideal balance of eye candy and history, best enjoyed under a canopy of trees and blue skies. Tour the parks, stop to smell the flowers, study the statuary, and picnic on the grass with a great bottle of wine. START: **Dumbarton Oaks garden entrance at 31st and R streets in Georgetown; no Metro access**

For an outdoor walking tour of Georgetown, see p 90.

1 ★★ **Dumbarton Oaks.** Enjoy the traditional French, Italian, and English gardens at this once-private home, now open to the public for tours. Discover bubbling fountains, stone archways, romantic hideaways, tiled pools, and even a Roman-style amphitheater. Flora includes an orangery, a rose garden, wisteria-covered arbors, groves of cherry trees, and

magnolias. When everything is in bloom, you can spend as long as an hour here. ⏲ 1 hr. 1703 32nd St. NW. ☎ 202/339-6410. www.doaks. org. $8 adults, $5 seniors and children. Gardens: Tues–Sun year-round; Mar 15–Oct 31 2–6pm; Nov 1–Mar 14 2–5pm (except national holidays and Dec 24).

2 ★ **Lover's Lane.** Follow the downhill, paved road that hugs Dumbarton Oaks's bricked wall next to Montrose Park. At the bottom, hang to the left and discover a gently cultivated enclave of gurgling brooks, weeping willow trees, wildflowers, and carefully placed benches for maximum romance and relaxation. ⏲ *20 min.*

③ ★ **Oak Hill Cemetery.** Reminiscent of Europe's historic cemeteries, the iron-gated, hilly grounds here are both beautifully kept and visually breathtaking. Spot a wild fox or a deer among the hundreds of 19th- and 20th-century headstones and the wealth of ornate statuary; stroll down toward the creek on winding paths as you tour yesterday's VIPs—and tell them to RIP. ⏲ *30 min. 30th and R sts. Mon–Fri 9am–4:30pm; closed to the public during funerals.*

Just off the corner of 30th and Q streets is ④ **Sara's Market,** a sweet, family-owned deli stocked with upscale treats. Choose from a small selection of prepared sandwiches in the cooler, or grab some British shortcakes, a snack bar,

Children playing in Dumbarton Oaks Park.

fresh fruit, a bag of nuts, and/or a decent bottle of wine to take with you into the great outdoors. *3008 Q St. NW (at 30th St.).*

Oak Hill Cemetery.

⑤ ★★ **Mount Vernon Trail.** Just across the river from downtown Georgetown, on Theodore Roosevelt Island, bikers, hikers, and joggers enter this scenic 18-mile (29km) trail. The path hugs the Virginia side of the Potomac River and offers breathtaking views of the classic monuments, memorials, and the river itself. Follow its course over bridges and through parks, and you'll eventually arrive at George Washington's historic Mount Vernon home (p 56). ⏲ *3 hr.* ☎ *703/ 289-2500. www.nps.gov/gwmp/ mtvernontrail.htm. Metro: Rosslyn.*

The **Mall & Tidal Basin**

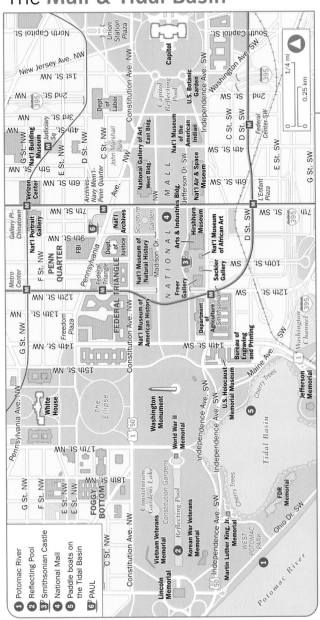

1 Potomac River
2 Reflecting Pool
3 Smithsonian Castle
4 National Mall
5 Paddle boats on the Tidal Basin
6 PAUL

Before it was the nation's capital, Washington, D.C. was a swamp. And if you wander the Mall and Tidal Basin in July or August, you'll have no trouble imagining what it was like, way back when. But few American urban environments can beat the Mall and Tidal Basin's outdoor appeal in spring, when Japanese cherry blossoms transform the cityscape, or in fall, with its perfect sweater weather. Throw in miles of bike and jogging paths in the heart of the city; botanical gardens; a galloping river; and plenty of green spaces, and you've got a rationale for avoiding the indoors. START: **Metro to Smithsonian**

Paddle boats on the Tidal Basin.

1 ★ **kids Stroll the Potomac River.** Whether you begin your walk in Georgetown, at Washington Harbour, or head toward the river near the Watergate Hotel or the Lincoln Memorial, spend some time promenading. You'll pass a legion of resident joggers; admire university crew teams sliding through the waves; catch grand glimpses of the memorials, monuments, and bridges; observe historic Georgetown from afar; pass 10 or more volleyball games in progress; picnic on the grass with kindred spirits inclined to stop and smell the roses; and root for fishermen who cast their rods in hopes of catching "the big one." On a beautiful day, nothing beats it. 🕐 *1 hr.*

Cherry Blossoms in Washington

Over 100 years ago in 1912, Tokyo gave Washington 3,000 delicately flowering, fragrant cherry trees in recognition of the growing friendship between the two cities. In 1965, Tokyo gave D.C. an additional 3,800 trees. Today, an estimated 700,000 travelers from all around the world arrive en masse every April, the peak of the cherry blossom season, to wander amid their vivid color and heady fragrance during the 2-week Cherry Blossom Festival. For a complete schedule of events, visit the official website, www.national cherryblossomfestival.org.

The Smithsonian Kite Festival on the National Mall.

❷ Reflect at the Reflecting Pool.

Pedestrian paths surround this ⅓-mile-long (.5km) body of water that visually connects the Lincoln Memorial and Washington Monument. It's also the site where thousands gathered to hear Rev. Martin Luther King, Jr. recite his legendary "I Have a Dream" speech in 1963. His followers stood around the pool—and in it—as they listened to the words that would change a nation. ⊘ *20 min.*

The ❸ ★★ **Smithsonian Castle**, just off the Mall on Independence Avenue, is an ideal spot to rest (if your dogs are barking) and to snack (if you're hungry like the wolf). It's also information central for the Smithsonian museums, so grab a sandwich or muffin and pick up a brochure to plan your next adventure. *1000 Jefferson Dr. SW. Daily 8:30am–5:30pm. Metro: Smithsonian. $–$$.*

❹ ★★★ kids Attend an event on the Mall.

Depending on the time of year when you arrive in Washington, you may stumble upon ethnic festivals, fireworks, kite-flying celebrations, dance performances, dedication ceremonies, children's workshops, orchestra concerts, holiday happenings, and much more on the National Mall. *Check out www. nps.gov/nama to find out what's happening during your visit.*

❺ ★ kids Rent paddle boats on the Tidal Basin.

Whether you're a kid or just a kid at heart, head to the Tidal Basin, weather permitting, and get ready to exercise your right to see the Jefferson Memorial while working up a sweat. ⊘ *1 hr. 2-passenger boat $12 per hr.; 4-passenger boat $19 per hr. Mar 15 to Labor Day daily 10am–6pm. Metro: Smithsonian Station (Blue/Orange lines; use the 12th St. and Independence Ave. exit). Walk west on Independence toward 15th St. Turn left on Raoul Wallenberg Place/15th St. and continue toward the Jefferson Memorial; look for the Tidal Basin Paddle Boat dock.*

Order a quiche and a macaroon to go at ❻ **PAUL,** a bustling French bistro and sidewalk cafe, and Parisian transplant right on Pennsylvania Avenue. *801 Pennsylvania Ave. NW. ☎ 202/524-4500. www.paul-usa.com. AE, DC, DISC, MC, V. Metro: Gallery Place/Chinatown or Archives. $–$$.* ●

The Best **Dining**

Capitol Hill & Penn Quarter Dining

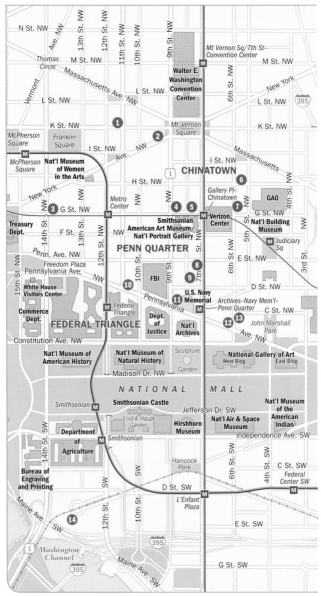

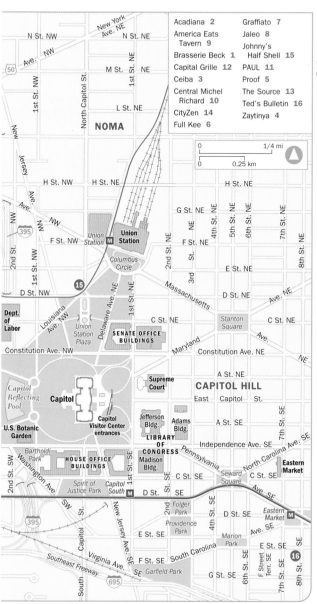

Acadiana **2**

America Eats
Tavern **9**

Brasserie Beck **1**

Capital Grille **12**

Ceiba **3**

Central Michel
Richard **10**

CityZen **14**

Full Kee **6**

Graffiato **7**

Jaleo **8**

Johnny's
Half Shell **15**

PAUL **11**

Proof **5**

The Source **13**

Ted's Bulletin **16**

Zaytinya **4**

Georgetown & Dupont Circle Dining

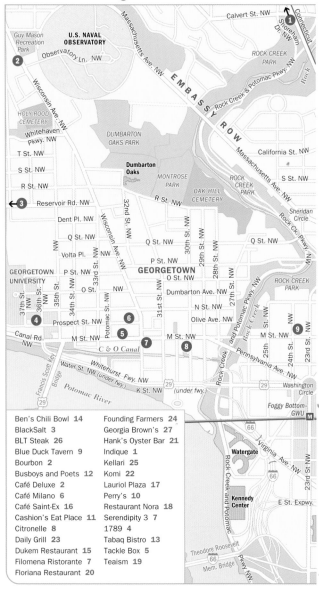

Ben's Chili Bowl **14**
BlackSalt **3**
BLT Steak **26**
Blue Duck Tavern **9**
Bourbon **2**
Busboys and Poets **12**
Café Deluxe **2**
Café Milano **6**
Café Saint-Ex **16**
Cashion's Eat Place **11**
Citronelle **8**
Daily Grill **23**
Dukem Restaurant **15**
Filomena Ristorante **7**
Floriana Restaurant **20**

Founding Farmers **24**
Georgia Brown's **27**
Hank's Oyster Bar **21**
Indique **1**
Kellari **25**
Komi **22**
Lauriol Plaza **17**
Perry's **10**
Restaurant Nora **18**
Serendipity 3 **7**
1789 **4**
Tabaq Bistro **13**
Tackle Box **5**
Teaism **19**

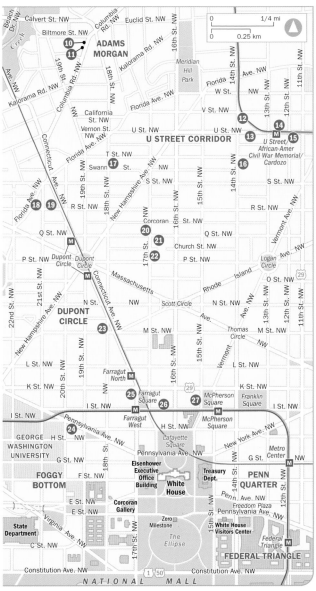

Dining Best Bets

Best Newcomer
★ Graffiato $$ *707 6th St. NW (p 139)*

Best Manhattan Rival
★★★ CityZen $$$$ *1330 Maryland Ave. SW (p 137)*

Best for Avoiding Carnivores
★ Founding Farmers $$ *1924 Pennsylvania Ave. NW (p 138)*

Best Hotel Eats
★★ Blue Duck Tavern $$ *24th and M sts. NW (p 135)*

Best Fussy French
★★★ Citronelle $$$$ *3000 M St. NW (p 137)*

Best Mussels and Beer
★★ Brasserie Beck $$ *1101 K St. NW (p 135)*

Best All-Organic
★★ Restaurant Nora $$$ *2132 Florida Ave. NW (p 141)*

Best for Under 10 Bucks
★★ Full Kee $ *509 H St. NW (p 138)*

Best Sexy Tapas Place
★★★ Zaytinya $$ *701 9th St. NW. (p 142)*

Best for Flirting with Elected Officials
★★★ Capital Grille $$$$ *601 Pennsylvania Ave. NW (p 137)*

Best for Winos
★★★ Proof $$$ *775 G St. NW. (p 141)*

Best for Blue Bloods
★ Café Milano $$$ *3251 Prospect St. NW (p 136)*

Best Fireside Dining
★★★ 1789 $$$$ *1226 36th St. NW (p 141)*

Tantalizing tapas at Zaytinya.

Best Fresh Fish
★★★ Kellari $$$ *4883 MacArthur Blvd. NW (p 140)*

Best for Moody Political Debates
★ Busboys and Poets *2021 14th St. NW (p 136)*

Best for Rowdy Rugrats
★★ Café Deluxe $$ *3228 Wisconsin Ave. NW (p 136)*

Best South of the Border
★ Lauriol Plaza $$ *1835 18th St. NW (p 140)*

Best Crab Cakes
★★★ BlackSalt $$$ *4883 MacArthur Blvd. NW (p 135)*

Best Historic Diner
★★ Ben's Chili Bowl $ *1213 U St. NW (p 135)*

Best Sweet Confections
★ Serendipity 3 $ *3150 M St. NW (p 141)*

Best for Expat Parisians
★★ PAUL $ *801 Pennsylvania Ave. NW (p 140)*

Restaurants A to Z

★★★ Acadiana DOWNTOWN
CAJUN New Orleans is still rebounding, but its legacy is strong here, in Cajun fare by Jeff Tunks, who cooked in the Big Easy for years. Try gumbo with andouille, crawfish pies, or fried okra in this upscale yet unfussy setting. *901 New York Ave. NW (K and 9th sts.).* ☎ *202/408-8848. www.acadiana restaurant.com. Entrees $21–$26. AE, DISC, MC, V. Lunch Mon–Fri; dinner Mon–Sat. Metro: Gallery Place/ Chinatown. Map p 130.*

★★ America Eats Tavern
DOWNTOWN *LATIN AMERICAN* Chef José Andrés claims to have made "American history on your plate," and you'll believe it when you peruse the menu, which features President Johnson's Brunswick Stew and oysters on the half shell. The restaurant even has a vintage soda fountain. *405 8th St. NW (D and E sts.).* ☎ *202/393-0812. www.americaeatstavern.com. Entrees $18–$24. AE, DC, DISC, MC, V. Lunch Mon–Fri; dinner Tues–Sun. Metro: Archives/Navy Memorial. Map p 130.*

★★ Ben's Chili Bowl U STREET
CORRIDOR *AMERICAN* Known for its Formica tables, sloppy chili dogs, and late-night banter, this old-time diner has drawn a who's who of African-American history since 1958—from Martin Luther King, Jr. to Redd Foxx to President Barack Obama. *1213 U St. NW (at 12th St.).* ☎ *202/667-0909. www.benschili bowl.com. Entrees $10. No credit cards. Mon–Sat breakfast, lunch & dinner; Sun lunch, dinner. Metro: Cardozo/U St. Map p 132.*

★★★ BlackSalt PALISADES *SEA-FOOD* Local seafood fans rave about chef Jeff Black's D.C. catch—this restaurant/fish market, with perfectly cooked black sea bass, fried Ipswich clams, crab cakes, fish stews, and more. *4883 MacArthur Blvd. NW (at V St.).* ☎ *202/342-9101. www.blacksaltrestaurant.com. Entrees $25–$35. DC, DISC, MC, V. Lunch Mon–Sat; dinner daily. No Metro access. Bus: B6. Map p 132.*

★ BLT Steak DOWNTOWN *AMERI-CAN* Despite its background as an upscale chain, the eatery serves quality steak with different sauces, and fish from the raw bar. The chef's warm popovers are just right. *1625 Eye St. NW.* ☎ *202/689-8999. www.bltsteak.com. Entrees $29–$45. AE, DISC, MC, V. Lunch Mon–Fri; dinner Mon–Sat. Metro: Farragut West. Map p 132.*

★★ Blue Duck Tavern DOWN-TOWN *AMERICAN* This downtown restaurant's comfortable American feel—hand-carved wooden benches and chairs, an inviting open kitchen, and a stellar menu—keeps Washingtonians coming back. *24th and M sts. NW.* ☎ *202/419-6755. www. blueducktavern.com. Entrees $13–$36. AE, MC, V. Breakfast daily; brunch Sat–Sun; lunch Mon–Fri; dinner daily. Metro: Foggy Bottom or Farragut North. Map p 132.*

★ Bourbon GLOVER PARK *AMERI-CAN* Young 20-somethings and Glover Park families flock to this consistently good restaurant for tater tots, burgers, and bourbon BBQ. *2348 Wisconsin Ave. NW.* ☎ *202/625-7770. www.bourbondc. com/home/gp. Entrees $8–$20. AE, DISC, MC, V. Lunch Sat–Sun; dinner daily. No Metro access. Map p 132.*

★★ Brasserie Beck DOWNTOWN *BELGIAN* Travel to Europe or head

Oysters at Brasserie Beck.

to this Belgian bistro for authentic brews and dishes such as steamed mussels, lamb sausage, roasted rabbit, and more than 50 beers. *1101 K St. NW.* ☎ *202/408-1717. www. beckdc.com. Entrees $23–$32. AE, DISC, MC, V. Brunch Sat–Sun; lunch Mon–Fri; dinner daily. Metro: Metro Center. Map p 130.*

★ kids **Busboys and Poets** 14TH STREET/LOGAN CIRCLE *AMERICAN* Local lit majors, groovy families, and budget fashionistas flock here for pizzas, burgers, and sandwiches, artfully prepared and affordable. *2021 14th St. NW (V St.).* ☎ *202/387-POET (7638). www.bus boysandpoets.com. Entrees $9–$17.*

AE, DC, DISC, MC, V. Breakfast, lunch & dinner daily. Metro: Cardozo/U St. Map p 132.

★★ kids **Café Deluxe** CATHEDRAL *AMERICAN* Can one bistro really serve all? Seems this one does: Guys hang out at the bar and watch sports. Families come early for the kids' menu and buckets of crayons. Foodies swear by the tuna steak sandwich. Everyone else enjoys the solid New American fare. *3228 Wisconsin Ave. NW (at Macomb St.).* ☎ *202/628-2233. www.cafedeluxe. com. Entrees $12–$20. AE, MC, V. Lunch Mon–Thurs & Sun; dinner Mon–Sun. No Metro access. Map p 132.*

★ **Café Milano** GEORGETOWN *ITALIAN* Pushy lobbyists, the society set, smug playboys, and ambitious young women in skimpy dresses don't flock here for the decent, but unremarkable, Italian food. They come to make the scene, close a deal, drink too much, touch the hems of power, and let loose, Washington-style, at this supercharged, always-packed restaurant and lounge. *3251 Prospect St. NW (at M St.).* ☎ *202/333-6183. www. cafemilano.net. Entrees $14–$42. AE, DC, DISC, MC, V. Lunch & dinner daily. Metro: Foggy Bottom or Roslyn. Map p 132.*

Café Saint-Ex, in 14th Street/U Street Corridor.

★★★ Café Saint-Ex 14TH STREET/
U STREET CORRIDOR *AMERICAN*
This Euro-chic bar and bistro serving
New American fare attracts goateed
hipsters and their supercilious
dates. A DJ spins in the lounge. *1847
14th St. NW (at T St.).* ☎ *202/265-
7839. www.saint-ex.com. Entrees
$15–$25. AE, DISC, MC, V. Lunch
Tues–Sun; dinner daily. Metro:
Cardozo/U St. Map p 132.*

★★★ Capital Grille PENN QUAR-
TER *AMERICAN* Cut through the
throng of short-skirted interns and
married officials at the bar—for
juicy steak and gossip from power
players talking too loudly at nearby
tables. *601 Pennsylvania Ave. NW
(at 6th St.).* ☎ *202/737-6200. www.
capitalgrille.com. Entrees $20–$45.
AE, DC, DISC, MC, V. Lunch Mon–Sat;
dinner daily. Metro: Archives/Navy
Memorial. Map p 130.*

★★ Cashion's Eat Place ADAMS
MORGAN *AMERICAN* Carnivores
roar with delight at this neighborhood mainstay, with its cramped yet
sophisticated interior. The mahogany bar will likely possess you to
order a martini with your buffalo
hanger steak. *1819 Columbia Rd.
NW (at the Biltmore).* ☎ *202/797-
1819. www.cashionseatplace.com.
Entrees $19–$35. MC, V. Dinner
Tues–Sat; brunch Sun. Metro: Adams
Morgan/Woodley Park. Map p 132.*

★★ Ceiba DOWNTOWN *LATIN
AMERICAN* If you love Latin American *ceviche* (think fresh tuna mari-
nated in lime and mango juice),
zingy mojitos, and fashion, book a
table at this outpost. *701 14th St.
NW (at G St.).* ☎ *202/393-3983.
www.ceibarestaurant.com. Entrees
$16–$29. AE, DC, DISC, MC, V. Lunch
Mon–Fri; dinner Mon–Sat. Metro:
Metro Center. Map p 130.*

★★ Central Michel Richard
DOWNTOWN *AMERICAN/FRENCH*
Citronelles casual, less expensive

Dinner at Ceiba.

brother, Central Michel Richard,
dishes out unstuffy fare such as
French onion soup, mussels, lobster
burgers, and soft shell crab. *1001
Pennsylvania Ave. NW.* ☎ *202/626-
0015. www.centralmichelrichard.
com. Entrees $16–$35. Lunch Mon–
Fri; dinner daily. Metro: Federal Triangle. Map p 130.*

★★★ Citronelle GEORGETOWN
FRENCH Fanatic foodies with cash
to burn: Make reservations now. Citronelle's white-jacketed waiters;
linen-dressed tables; and delicate
foie gras carpaccio, caviar penguins,
and squab (served three ways)
won't disappoint. *3000 M St. NW
(at 30th St.).* ☎ *202/625-2150.
www.citronelledc.com. Dinner
entrees $85–$150. AE, DC, MC, V.
Breakfast & dinner daily. Metro:
Foggy Bottom. Map p 132.*

★★★ CityZen WASHINGTON HAR-
BOUR *AMERICAN* In the posh Mandarin Oriental Hotel, Chef Eric
Ziebold—formerly of The French
Laundry, and voted "Best Mid-Atlan-
tic Chef" by James Beard in 2008—
makes gourmands swoon with his
adventurous cuisine (think black

bass and rabbit loin). *1330 Maryland Ave. SW (at 12th St.).* ☎ *202/787-6148. www.mandarinoriental.com. Entrees $75–$125. AE, DC, DISC, MC, V. Dinner Tues–Sat. Metro: Smithsonian. Map p 130.*

★★ kids **Daily Grill** DUPONT CIRCLE *AMERICAN* With several locations, this Washington staple is perfect for a quick lunch or dinner with kids, whether you're craving a burger and fries or seared salmon and baked potato. Enjoy roomy booths and an after-work bar scene. *1200 18th St. NW (Connecticut Ave.).* ☎ *202/822-5282. www.dailygrill.com. Entrees $16–$30. AE, DC, DISC, MC, V. Lunch & dinner daily. Metro: Dupont Circle. Map p 132.*

★ **Dukem Restaurant** U STREET *ETHIOPIAN* D.C. is known for its flourishing Ethiopian population. Diners looking for an authentic taste of the culture need look no further than this popular downtown restaurant, offering traditional *sambusa, kitfo,* and *injera,* and a large variety of vegetarian options. *1114–1118 U St., NW.* ☎ *202/667-8735. www.dukemrestaurant.com. Entrees $12–$29. AE, MC, V. Lunch & dinner daily. Metro: U Street/Cardozo. Map p 132.*

★★ **Filomena Ristorante** GEORGETOWN *ITALIAN* You won't walk away disappointed—or hungry—from this Italian favorite in Georgetown. Portions are large enough for two, service is always great, and admiring the tacky decorations will keep you entertained long after your food has arrived. *1063 Wisconsin Ave. NW.* ☎ *202/338-8800. www.filomenadc.com. Entrees $22–$42. AE, DISC, MC, V. Lunch & dinner daily; brunch Sun. No Metro access. Map p 132.*

★ **Floriana Restaurant** DUPONT CIRCLE *ITALIAN* Tucked away in a historic Dupont town house, this restaurant makes you feel as if

Ethiopian cuisine at Dukem Restaurant.

you're dining in someone's very nice living room. It features some of the best Italian in the city, too: Think butternut squash ravioli and truffle risotto. *1602 17th St. NW.* ☎ *202/667-5937. www.florianarestaurant.com. Entrees $15–$27. AE, MC, V. Dinner daily; brunch Sat–Sun. Metro: Dupont Circle. Map p 132.*

★ **Founding Farmers** DOWNTOWN *AMERICAN* True to its name, this restaurant celebrates the American farmer, serving sustainably farmed, grown, and harvested foods. The heartland-inspired menu rotates seasonally, depending on what's available. *1924 Pennsylvania Ave. NW.* ☎ *202/822-8783. www.wearefoundingfarmers.com. Entrees: $20–$30. Lunch & dinner daily; brunch Sat–Sun. Metro: Foggy Bottom. Map p 132.*

★★ **Full Kee** CHINATOWN *ASIAN* The city's best chefs eat here on their days off (Eric Zeibold is a fan). Try the Hong Kong–style shrimp dumpling soup, oyster casserole, or any stir-fry. Open late. *509 H St. NW (at 6th St.).* ☎ *202/371-2233. www.fullkeedc.com. Entrees $10. No credit cards. Lunch & dinner daily. Metro: Gallery Place/Chinatown. Map p 130.*

Georgia Brown's DOWNTOWN *SOUTHERN* The dining room may

seem formal, but the food is fit for a down-home, Southern jubilee: golden-fried chicken; cornmeal-crusted catfish fingers; shrimp and grits; and sweet, crunchy, fried okra. *950 15th St. NW (at K St.).* ☎ *202/393-4499. www.gbrowns.com. Entrees $17–$26. AE, DC, DISC, MC, V. Lunch Mon–Fri; dinner daily; brunch Sun. Metro: Farragut North. Map p 132.*

★ **Graffiato** GALLERY PLACE *ITALIAN* Former Top Chef star Mike Isabella recently opened this Italian-inspired restaurant, which has quickly become a go-to spot for authentic hand-cut spaghetti, potato gnocchi, and pizzas. *707 6th St. NW.* ☎ *202/289-3600. www.graffiatodc. com. Entrees $10–$20. AE, MC, V. Lunch & dinner daily. Metro: Gallery Place/Chinatown. Map p 130.*

★★ **Hank's Oyster Bar** DUPONT CIRCLE *SEAFOOD* Chef-owner Jamie Leeds mismatched the furnishings in this homey space so it wouldn't be "too perfect" a setting for beer, oysters, lobster rolls, and the like. *1624 Q St. NW (at 17th St.).* ☎ *202/462-4265. www.hanksdc. com. Entrees $12–$19. AE, MC, V. Dinner daily; lunch Fri–Sun. Metro: Dupont Circle. Map p 132.*

★ **Indique** CLEVELAND PARK *INDIAN* Curry, naan, biriyani. All of the flavors of India are here at this chic two-floor restaurant known for its consistently good food. *3512 Connecticut Ave. NW.*

Dinner at Graffiato.

A seafood sandwich at Hank's Oyster Bar.

☎ *202/244-6600. www.indique.com. Lunch Fri–Sun; dinner daily. $14–$19. AE, DC, DISC, MC, V. Metro: Cleveland Park. Map p 132.*

★ **Jaleo** PENN QUARTER *SPANISH* Chef José Andrés started the "small plates" revolution in Washington with this sexy, casual tapas bar and restaurant in the heart of Penn Quarter. *480 7th St. NW (at E St.).* ☎ *202/628-7949. www.jaleo.com. Entrees $16–$18; tapas $3.25–$9.95. AE, DC, DISC, MC, V. Lunch & dinner daily; brunch Sat–Sun. Metro: Gallery Place/Chinatown. Map p 130.*

TIP

If a place beckons, call ahead for reservations, especially on a Saturday night. You can often reserve your table online at www.open table.com. If you wait until the last minute to make a reservation, expect to dine early or very late—say 5:30 to 6pm or after 9:30pm.

★ kids **Johnny's Half Shell** CAPITOL HILL *SEAFOOD* Maryland is famous for its crab cakes, and this small, no-frills neighborhood restaurant cooks them with loads of meat and very little filler. Casual and kid-friendly. *400 N. Capitol St. NW (at Louisiana Ave.).* ☎ *202/737-0400. www.johnnyshalfshell.net. Entrees $7.50–$24. AE, MC, V. Breakfast Tues–Fri; lunch Mon–Fri; dinner Mon–Sat. Metro: Dupont Circle. Map p 130.*

The Best Dining

A Seat at the Bar

Most D.C. restaurants require reservations, and in this cutthroat town, all the best seem always to be booked. What's a hungry, reservation-less foodie to do? Head to the bar, of course. In an effort to please those who haven't managed to reserve a table in their main dining rooms, but who nevertheless hope to sample some of their food, a number of the city's top restaurants have started serving modified versions of their regular menus at the bar. The experience often proves more intimate and convivial than that in the main dining room, and here's the kicker: It's always less expensive.

–Elise Hartman Ford

★★★ **Kellari** DOWNTOWN. *GREEK* Prepare for an expensive dinner here, but it will be worth it, especially if you hand-pick your fresh fish, which has been flown in from Spain or Greece that day. Spanakopita and *Saganaki,* the traditional flaming Graviera cheese, are the real deal at this taverna. *1700 K St. NW.* ☎ *202/535-5274. www.kellaridc.com. Entrees: $25 and up. AE, MC, V. Lunch & dinner daily; brunch Sat–Sun. Metro: Farragut North. Map p 132.*

★★ **Komi** DUPONT CIRCLE *AMERICAN* Wow: Chef Johnny Monis's savory Mediterranean cooking, homemade breads, and light, lively desserts. The tiny dining room is casual, the service perfect. Worth the wait. *1509 17th St. NW (near P St.).* ☎ *202/332-9200. www.komirestaurant.com. Tasting menu $135 per person; wine pairing $70. AE, MC, V. Dinner Tues–Sat. Metro: Dupont Circle. Map p 132.*

★ **Lauriol Plaza** DUPONT CIRCLE *MEXICAN* Is this multilevel place ever not packed to the roof, where singles flirt and drink? The Mexican fare is worth its salt—as are the strong margaritas. *1835 18th St. NW (at S St.).* ☎ *202/387-0035. www.lauriolplaza.com. Entrees $6.50–$16. AE, DC, DISC, MC, V. Brunch Sat–Sun;* lunch daily; dinner Mon–Sat. Metro: Dupont Circle. Map p 132.

★★ kids **PAUL** DOWNTOWN *FRENCH* A sliver of a cafe, with lovely, brisk sandwiches, quiches, and confections. Expat Parisians camp out here. *801 Pennsylvania Ave. NW.* ☎ *202/524-4500. www.paul-usa.com. Entrees $10–$15. AE, DISC, MC, V. Breakfast, lunch & dinner daily. Metro: Gallery Place/Chinatown. Map p 131.*

★★ **Perry's** ADAMS MORGAN *AMERICAN* One of the busiest rooftop scenes in the city, Perry's has been long famous for its Sunday drag brunch. Everyone from GW students to 40-somethings collide here for a diverse menu of crusty crab cakes, sushi, pork schnitzel, mussels and more. *1811 Columbia Rd. NW.* ☎ *202/234-6218. www.perrysadamsmorgan.com. Brunch Sun; lunch Sat;*

Dinner at Proof.

Dessert at 1789.

dinner daily. $12–$20. AE, DISC, MC, V. Metro: Woodley Park–Zoo/Adams Morgan. Map p 132.

★★★ **Proof** PENN QUARTER *AMERICAN* Choose from some 1,000 bottles of wine, or off a rolling champagne cart, then dine on freshly prepared contemporary dishes that make a nod toward eco-friendly cuisine. *775 G St. NW.* ☎ *202/737-7663. www.proofdc.com. Entrees $24–$29. AE, MC, V. Lunch Tues–Fri; dinner daily. Metro: Gallery Place/Chinatown. Map p 130.*

★★ **Restaurant Nora** DUPONT CIRCLE *ORGANIC* An early advocate of fresh, seasonal ingredients, chef-owner Nora Pouillon's freerange chicken and tender roasted pork are a testament to how good a simple, organic meal can be. There's a great wine list, too. *2132 Florida Ave. NW (at R St.).* ☎ *202/462-5143. www.noras.com. Entrees $24–$32. AE, MC, V. Dinner Mon–Sat. Metro: Dupont Circle. Map p 132.*

★ **Serendipity 3** GEORGETOWN *DESSERTS* Sure, it has regular food, too, but the chocolate brownie sundaes and deep-fried Oreos take center stage at this straight-from-New York outpost. For $1,000, you can order the Golden Opulence, the world's most expensive sundae. *3150 M St. NW.* ☎ *202/333-5193. www.serendipity3dc.com. Entrees $15–$20. AE, DISC, MC, V. Breakfast, lunch & dinner Mon–Sat; brunch Sun. No Metro access. Bus: DC Circulator. Map p 132.*

---

one's for you. Evoking a classic beach shack with communal tables and chalkboard menus, Tackle Box offers the best seafood without the fuss. *3245 M St. NW. ☎ 202/337-TBOX (337-8269). Entrees $9–$13. AE, DC, MC, V. Lunch & dinner daily. No Metro access (See "Traveling to Georgetown," on p 91). Map p 132.*

★ **kids Teaism** DUPONT CIRCLE *ASIAN* Eavesdrop on moody political debates inside as you sup on healthy noodle dishes and baked goods. *2009 R St. NW (Connecticut Ave. and 21st St.). ☎ 202/667-3827. www.teaism.com. Entrees $1.50–$10. AE, MC, V. Breakfast, lunch & dinner daily. Metro: Dupont Circle. Map p 132.*

★★ **Ted's Bulletin** CAPITOL HILL *AMERICAN* Extra, extra! Read all about it at this fun Barracks Row restaurant that features newspapers for menus and some of the city's best comfort food. Don't leave without trying one of their famous milkshakes or pop tarts. *505 8th St.*

Tapas at Zaytinya, in Penn Quarter.

SE. ☎ 202/544-8337. www.teds bulletin.com. Entrees $15–$25. AE, MC, V. Breakfast, lunch & dinner daily. Metro: Eastern Market. Map p 130.

★★★ **Zaytinya** PENN QUARTER *MIDDLE EASTERN* Zaytinya is a must for fans of tapas-style dining—with its soaring ceilings, white-washed walls, communal tables shared by beautiful people, and modern Middle Eastern mezze. *701 9th St. NW (at G St.). ☎ 202/638-0800. www.zaytinya.com. Entrees $18–$23. AE, DC, DISC, MC, V. Lunch & dinner daily. Metro: Gallery Place/Chinatown. Map p 130. ●*

Mobile Eats

One can say many things about Washington, but one thing is definitely true: When we find something we like, we stick to it. The trend in food trucks serving a variety of ethnic and healthy tastes is no exception. Keep an eye out for **Fogol Brothers,** which serves up curry and butter chicken as well as vegetarian options like palak paneer. You'll find sweet and savory pie slices at **DCPieTruck**, the roving counterpart of local pie shop Dangerously Delicious Pies on H Street. And as the name implies, the **Red Hook Lobster Truck** dishes out delicious Maine-style lobster rolls for $15. Track them all via Twitter or visit www.foodtruckfiesta.com to find their current locations.

As in many cities across the U.S., the food truck movement is all the rage in D.C.

D.C. **Nightlife**

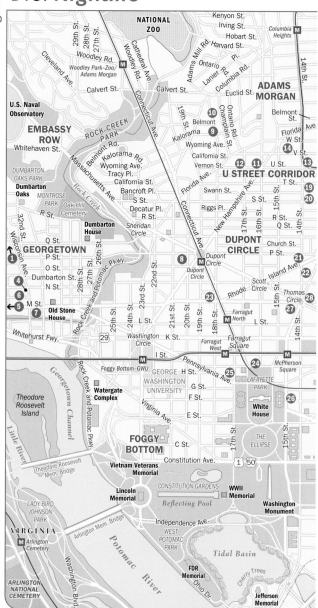

Previous page: Eighteenth Street Lounge.

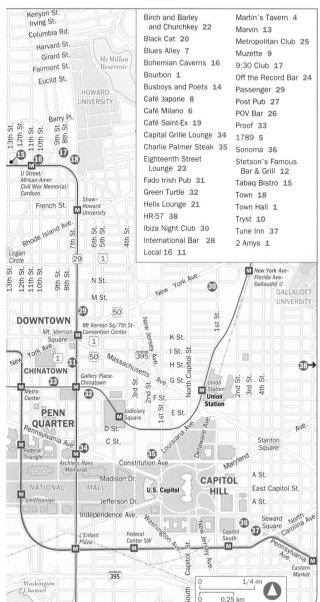

Birch and Barley
  and Churchkey 22
Black Cat 20
Blues Alley 7
Bohemian Caverns 16
Bourbon 1
Busboys and Poets 14
Café Japone 8
Café Milano 6
Café Saint-Ex 19
Capital Grille Lounge 34
Charlie Palmer Steak 35
Eighteenth Street
  Lounge 23
Fado Irish Pub 31
Green Turtle 32
Helix Lounge 21
HR-57 38
Ibiza Night Club 30
International Bar 28
Local 16 11

Martin's Tavern 4
Marvin 13
Metropolitan Club 25
Muzette 9
9:30 Club 17
Off the Record Bar 24
Passenger 29
Post Pub 27
POV Bar 26
Proof 33
1789 5
Sonoma 36
Stetson's Famous
  Bar & Grill 12
Tabaq Bistro 15
Town 18
Town Hall 1
Tryst 10
Tune Inn 37
2 Amys 1

Nightlife Best Bets

Best for **Hopheads**
★★ Birch and Barley and Churchkey, *1337 14th St. NW (p 147)*

Best for Watching Interns **Flirt with Elected Officials**
★ Charlie Palmer Steak, *101 Constitution Ave. NW (p 150)*

Best for Rubbing Shoulders with **Capitol Hillers**
★ Tune Inn, *331½ Pennsylvania Ave. NE (p 151)*

Best for **Wine & Romance**
★★★ 1789, *1226 36th St. NW (p 152)*

Best for Overhearing **State Secrets**
★★ Off the Record Bar, *Hay-Adams Hotel, 800 16th St. NW (p 151)*

Best for **Scotch & Cigar Lovers**
★ Capital Grille Lounge, *601 Pennsylvania Ave. NW (p 150)*

Best for **Live Jazz & Blues**
★ Blues Alley, *1073 Wisconsin Ave. NW (p 149)*

Best for Catching **Indie Acts**
★ 9:30 Club, *815 V St. NW (p 149)*

Best **Private Power Club**
★★ Metropolitan Club, *1700 H St. NW (p 150)*

Best for Spotting *Post* **Reporters**
★★ Post Pub, *1422 L St. NW (p 151)*

Best for **Drinks While the Kids Eat Pizza**
★★ 2 Amys, *3715 Macomb St. NW (p 147)*

Best for Mingling with **Socialites**
★ Café Milano, *3252 Prospect St. NW (p 151)*

Best **Literary/Artsy-Fartsy Haunt**
★ Busboys and Poets, *2021 14th St. NW (p 147)*

Best for Waiting Behind the **Velvet Ropes**
★★ Ibiza Night Club, *1222 First St. NE (p 152)*

Best for **Monumental Views**
★ POV Bar, W Hotel, *515 15th St. NW (p 150)*

Best **Rooftop Drinking**
Local 16, *1602 U St. NW (p 150)*

Best **Dive Bar**
★ Stetson's Famous Bar & Grill, *1610 U St. NW (p 147)*

Best for **Grapeheads**
★★ Proof, *775 G St., NW (p 152)*

Tip

Metro trains run until 3am on weekends, and special shuttle service also goes to Adams Morgan (home to lots of clubs, but no Metro stops). Take the Metro to the Red Line's Woodley Park–Zoo/Adams Morgan station or to the Green Line's U Street–Cardozo station, and hop on the no. 98 Adams Morgan–U Street Link Shuttle, which travels through Adams Morgan, between these two stations, after 6pm daily except Saturday, when service starts at 10am. The U Link Shuttle operates every 15 minutes and costs only 25¢.

Nightlife A to Z

Beer Lovers/Casual

★★ Birch and Barley and Churchkey DUPONT CIRCLE   A multilevel bar and a selection of more than 50 drafts plus 500 bottles makes this restaurant a pilgrimage site for brew lovers. *1337 14th St. NW.* ☎ *202/567-2576. www.birchand barley.com. Metro: Dupont Circle.*

★ Fado Irish Pub PENN QUARTER This authentic Irish watering hole has a vintage taste of the Emerald Isle, from vintage tables and chairs to the huge stones that make up the walls and floors, plus pints of Guinness on tap. The din here is at 10 decibels, the pub grub is savory, and the music is live. *808 7th St. NW (at H St.).* ☎ *202/789-0066. www. fadoirishpub.com. Metro: Gallery Place/Chinatown.*

★ Stetson's Famous Bar & Grill U STREET CORRIDOR   Shoot some pool with your pals over draft ale at this neighborhood pub with a respectable mix of classic rock on the jukebox, charmingly dated decor, and an outdoor patio for mellow summer nights. *1610 U St. NW (at 16th St.).* ☎ *202/667-6295. www.stetsons-dc.com. Metro: U St. Corridor.*

★ Town Hall GLOVER PARK   A new location and a revamped interior have revitalized this D.C. landmark, whose casual food and drink menu is reliably good. *2340 Wisconsin Ave. NW.* ☎ *202/333-5640. www. townhalldc.com. No Metro Access.*

Family Spirits

★★ 2 Amys GLOVER PARK   Mom and Dad, you need a drink, and the rugrats are hungry. So take them out for authentic Neapolitan pizza while you savor a lovely glass of Italian red wine. *3715 Macomb St. NW (at Wisconsin Ave.).* ☎ *202/885-5700. www.2amyspizza.com. Metro: Tenleytown/AU.*

Gay & Lesbian

★ Town U STREET CORRIDOR Wild nights are the norm at this high-energy dance club that has an outdoor smoking area, two levels, and video screens, and stays open until 4am. *2009 8th St. NW.* ☎ *202/234-TOWN (8696). www.towndc.com. Cover $12–$20. Metro: U Street/ Cardozo.*

Hipster Haunts

★ Busboys and Poets 14TH STREET   Local lit majors and broke fashionistas flock here for pizzas, burgers, and booze. Prices won't break the bank. *2021 14th St. NW (at U St.).* ☎ *202/387-7638. www. busboysandpoets.com. AE, MC, V. Metro: Cardozo/U St.*

Café Saint-Ex 14TH STREET Named for the author of *Le Petit Prince,* this Eurochic bar and bistro serving New American fare attracts goateed hipsters and their supercilious dates. A DJ spins in the downstairs lounge. *1847 14th St. NW (at T St.).* ☎ *202/265-7839. Metro: Cardozo/U St.*

★★ Helix Lounge LOGAN CIRCLE Funky, pop-centric decor plus colorful cocktails and a nice outdoor space make this retro-cool lounge in the Hotel Helix a hangout among Washington's scene-makers. *1430 Rhode Island Ave. NW (at 14th St.).* ☎ *202/462-9001. Metro: McPherson Sq. or Dupont Circle.*

★ **Marvin** 14TH STREET   When you arrive, head to the upstairs deck where locals mingle, discuss politics, and drink a selection of craft beers. *2007 14th St., NW (at U St.).* ☎ *202/797-7171. www.marvin dc.com. AE, MC, V. Metro: Cardozo/ U St.*

★ **Passenger** PENN QUARTER Service can be slow here, but that's only because bartenders put so much concentration into making their eclectic cocktails featuring fresh herbs and different liquors, outlined on a chalkboard above the bar each night. *1021 7th St. NW.* ☎ *202/393-0220. www.passengerdc.com. Metro: Gallery Place/Chinatown.*

★ **Tabaq Bistro** U STREET CORRI-DOR   The decor is minimalist, with geometric shapes, sharp edges, and red tones. The glass-paneled terrace yields great views of the city. The people-watching is colorful. And, if that's not enough, come for the "hookah" menu. *1336 U St. NW (at 13th St.).* ☎ *202/265-0965. www. tabaqdc.com. Metro: Cardozo/U St.*

Tryst ADAMS MORGAN   Part coffeehouse, part playground, part gallery, part pick-up lounge, and part study hall, Tryst is all things for most Adams Morganers. Early to open and late to close, this always-buzzing gathering spot is the place to ogle original art, eat a sandwich or score a scone, groove to live music, or journal furiously while downing an English ale. *Coffeehouse: 2459 18th St. NW (at Columbia Rd.).* ☎ *202/232-5500. www.trystdc.com. Mon–Wed 6:30am–midnight; Fri–Sat 6:30am–3am; Thurs 6:30am–2am; Sun 7am–midnight. Metro: Woodley Park–Zoo/Adams Morgan.*

Karaoke

★★ **Café Japone** DUPONT CIR-CLE   If you like singing for your supper or just belting out a Broadway tune, look no further than this local institution for sushi-loving *American Idol* rejects and pitch-perfect exhibitionists. *2032 P St. NW (at 21st St.).* ☎ *202/223-2573. www.japonedc.com. Metro: Dupont Circle.*

★★ **Muzette** ADAMS MORGAN Those who only want to embarrass themselves in front of friends and not a bar full of strangers should rent a room at Muzette. You'll find a

Helix Lounge.

Tryst, in Adams Morgan.

great song selection and tasty Korean dishes to accompany your solo act. *2305 18th St. NW (btw. N. Kalorama and N. Belmont Rd.)* ☎ *202/758-2971. www.muzette. com. Metro: Adams Morgan.*

Live Music
★★ **Black Cat** 14th STREET Faded punk rockers, still riding on the Sex Pistols' glory days, gather here to vet a new generation of mohawked wonders, and to check out other national and international alternative acts. *1811 14th St. NW (btw. S & T sts.).* ☎ *202/667-7960. www.blackcatdc.com. Cover $5–$20 for concerts; no cover in Red Room Bar. Metro: Cardozo/U St.*

★ **Blues Alley** GEORGETOWN The *New York Times* once called this place "the nation's finest jazz and supper club." Indeed, its reputation is deserved, if only for its Cajun-infused fare and performances by legends like Eartha Kitt and Mary Wilson. *1073 Wisconsin Ave. NW (at M St.).* ☎ *202/337-4141. www.blues alley.com. Cover $16–$75, plus $10 food and drink minimum, plus $2.25 surcharge. Metro: Foggy Bottom then Georgetown Metro Connection Shuttle.*

★★ **Bohemian Caverns** U STREET CORRIDOR Calling itself the "sole home of soul jazz," this legendary joint has attracted A-list artists (Duke Ellington and Miles Davis among them) for decades. Its keyboard awning greets you, and its creative cavelike interior is like no other. *2001 11th St. NW (at U St.).* ☎ *202/299-0801. www.bohemian caverns.com. $10 cover Fri–Sat; no food and drink minimum. Entrees $7.95–$19. Metro: Cardozo/U St.*

HR-57 LOGAN CIRCLE This tiny jazz house that doubles as a non-profit for music preservation is the real deal. Grab a shabby chair in the brick-walled club to listen to amateur and professional artists jam into the night. You can BYOB for a $3 corking fee, or purchase wine and beer by the glass. *816 H St. NE.* ☎ *202/253-0044. www.hr57.org. No Metro access.*

★ **9:30 Club** U STREET CORRIDOR Fans of '80s warblers Bob Mould and 'Ments frontman Paul Westerberg will love this intimate den for independent music. It boasts the best acoustic and low-fi sets on the East Coast. *815 V St. NW (at Vermont Ave.).* ☎ *202/265-0930. www.930.com. Tickets $10–$50 in advance. Metro: Cardozo/U St.*

Black Cat.

Outdoor/Rooftop

International Bar DOWN-TOWN   Come for the classic cocktails in this lobby bar of the Washington Plaza Hotel, and then move outdoors to the poolside terrace and lounge, one of the only outdoor pool scenes in the D.C. area. *10 Thomas Circle NW.* ☎ *202/842-1300. www.washington plazahotel.com. Metro: McPherson Square.*

Local 16 U STREET CORRIDOR You might feel you're at a crowded house party in this renovated town house turned bar that also happens to have one of the best rooftops for happy-hour mingling, dining, and drinking. *1602 U St. NW.* ☎ *202/265-2828. www.localsixteen.com. Metro: U Street/Cardozo.*

★ **POV Bar** DOWNTOWN   Order a martini and take in the view of the Washington Monument and the National Mall and glimpses of the White House from this swanky bar in the W Hotel. *515 15th St. NW.* ☎ *202/ 661-2400. www.wwashingtondc. com/POVRoofTerrace. Metro: Metro Center.*

Political Intrigue

★ **Capital Grille Lounge** PENN QUARTER   The premier political watering hole in town, this clubby lounge is witness to power-brokering, scandals, and plenty of cigar-tinged intrigue—plus premium whiskeys and 300 wines on its regular list. *601 Pennsylvania Ave. NW (at 6th St.).* ☎ *202/737-6200. www. thecapitalgrille.com. Metro: Archives/Navy Memorial.*

★ **Charlie Palmer Steak** DOWN-TOWN   The city's elegant outpost for this nationally acclaimed chef attracts the town's top political dogs for stiff drinks and perfectly prepared sirloins. *101 Constitution Ave. NW (at Louisiana Ave.).* ☎ *202/547-8100. www.charlie palmer.com. Metro: Union Station.*

★ **Martin's Tavern** GEORGETOWN Chris Matthews, Tucker Carlson, and every president since Harry Truman have come to this "Old Washington" pub. Sidle up to the mahogany bar for a Scotch or take a seat in one of its booths, like the one where JFK proposed to Jackie. *1264 Wisconsin Ave. NW.* ☎ *202/333-7370. www.martins-tavern.com. No Metro access (see box, p 91).*

★★ **Metropolitan Club** DOWN-TOWN   In a circa-1908 building listed on the National Register of Historic Places, this posh club attracts D.C.'s movers and shakers.

1700 H St. NW (at 17th St.). ☎ 202/835-2500. www.metroclub.org. Metro: Farragut North or Farragut West.

★★ **Off the Record Bar** DOWNTOWN   Billed as "Washington's place to be seen and not heard," Off the Record was selected by *Forbes* as one of the "World's Best Hotel Bars" in July 2004. It's just steps from the White House; I wish its red-paneled walls could talk. *In the Hay-Adams Hotel: 800 16th St. NW (at H St.). ☎ 202/638-6600. www.hay adams.com. Metro: McPherson Sq.*

★★ **Post Pub** DOWNTOWN   If you want to run into today's versions of Bob Woodward and Carl Bernstein, look no further than this tiny relic of a bar. It serves draft beer and belly-filling grub to *Post* staffers, who work just around the corner. *1422 L St. NW (at Vermont Ave.). ☎ 202/628-2111. www.post pubdc.com. Metro: McPherson Sq.*

★ **Tune Inn** CAPITOL HILL   A great happy hour and an eclectic dive bar vibe attract the just-out-of-college-and-working-on-the-Hill set, who down boozy beverages as they diss their famous bosses. *331½ Pennsylvania Ave. NE. ☎ 202/543-2725. www.tuneinndc.com. Metro: Union Station.*

Sports

★★ **Green Turtle** PENN QUARTER Gilbert Arenas fans, this is your hot spot for catching NBA hoops on big-screen TVs, as well as all major sporting events, from Wimbledon to the Super Bowl. *601 F St. NW. ☎ 202/637-8889. www.thegreen turtle.com. Metro: Gallery Place/Chinatown.*

VIP Scene

★ **Café Milano** GEORGETOWN Rub shoulders with Botoxed social-ites, back-slapping senators, and European playboys at the lively bar, or sit down for a meal of middling-to-good Italian fare—if you can get a table. *3251 Prospect St. NW (at Potomac). ☎ 202/333-6183. www.cafemilano.net. Metro: Foggy Bottom or Rosslyn.*

Eighteenth Street Lounge DUPONT CIRCLE   Some would say this multilevel meeting place has seen its day. But it continues to draw crowds and beautiful people through its unmarked front door, to mingle on salon-style sofas and groove to live music. *1212 18th St. NW (at Connecticut Ave.). ☎ 202/696-0210. Cover: $5–$20 Tues–Sun. Metro: Farragut North.*

The rooftop scene at Local 16.

National Harbor

If you're willing to make a day and night of it, hop a cab to **National Harbor,** another entertainment outpost, just a few miles from downtown D.C. Here, you'll find shops, nearly 20 restaurants, and a dueling piano bar along the newly constructed streets. The immense Gaylord National Hotel is the centerpiece, and features a seafood eatery, an acclaimed steak restaurant, more stores, and a Bellagio-type fountain that shoots 60 feet (18m) in the air. Call ☎ **877/628-5427** or visit www.nationalharbor.com for details.

★★ **Ibiza Night Club** DOWN-TOWN   This hopping nightclub is packed with young people downing shots, getting their groove on, and taking twirls around dance floor. *1222 First St. NE. ☎ 888/424-9232. www.ibizadc.com. Thurs–Sat. Metro: New York Avenue.*

Whiskey Lovers
★★ **Bourbon** GLOVER PARK   Named for the 50 Kentucky bourbons (and assorted Tennessee varieties) poured here, this casual, modern pub attracts sports fans, slumming hipsters, grad students— even neighborhood families, who dine upstairs on tasty burgers and crab cakes. *2348 Wisconsin Ave. NW (near Calvert St.). ☎ 202/625-7770. www.bourbondc.com. No Metro access.*

The vast selection at Bourbon.

Wine Lovers
★★ **Proof** PENN QUARTER   More than 1,000 different bottles, some from the owner's private collection, and an Enomatic wine system that dispenses perfect pours by the glass make this trendy spot a must-visit for oenophiles. *775 G St. NW. ☎ 202/737-7663. www.proofdc. com. Metro: Gallery Place/China-town.*

★★★ **1789** GEORGETOWN   A new chef isn't the only attraction at this Washington mainstay. This low-lit, classic New American restaurant has a very romantic bar and one of the city's most impressive wine lists. *1226 36th St. NW (at Prospect St.). ☎ 202/965-1789. www.1789 restaurant.com. No Metro access (see box, p 91).*

★★ **Sonoma** CAPITOL HILL   The hot spot on the Hill, serving Mediterranean small plates with more than 35 well-chosen wines by the bottle. Be prepared to get friendly with strangers; the place is always packed and tables are *thisclose. 223 Pennsylvania Ave. SE (at 2nd St.). ☎ 202/544-8088. www.sonomadc. com. Metro: Capitol South.* ●

9 The Best Arts & Entertainment

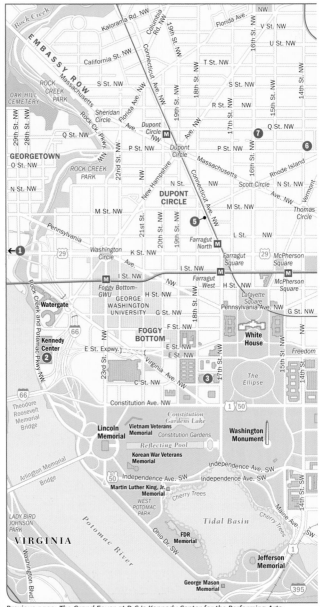

Previous page: The Grand Foyer at D.C.'s Kennedy Center for the Performing Arts.

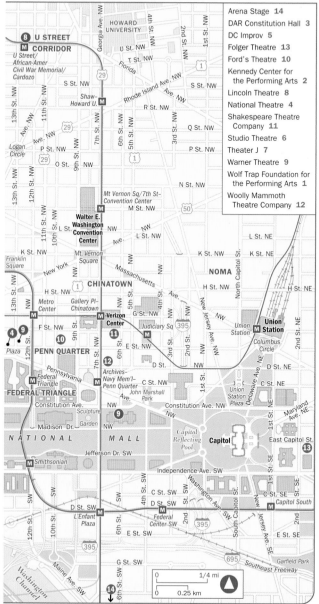

Arena Stage **14**
DAR Constitution Hall **3**
DC Improv **5**
Folger Theatre **13**
Ford's Theatre **10**
Kennedy Center for
  the Performing Arts **2**
Lincoln Theatre **8**
National Theatre **4**
Shakespeare Theatre
  Company **11**
Studio Theatre **6**
Theater J **7**
Warner Theatre **9**
Wolf Trap Foundation for
  the Performing Arts **1**
Woolly Mammoth
  Theatre Company **12**

Arts & Entertainment **Best Bets**

Studio Theatre, in 14th Street/Logan Circle.

Best **Restored Theater**
★ Lincoln Theatre, *1215 U St. NW (p 157)*

Best for **History Buffs**
★★ Ford's Theatre, *511 10th St. NW (p 157)*

Best for **High-Brow Performance**
★★★ Kennedy Center for the Performing Arts, *2700 F St. NW (p 157)*

Best for **Avant-Garde Acts**
★★ Woolly Mammoth Theatre Company, *641 D St. NW (p 158)*

Best Place to **Laugh So Hard You Cry**
★★ DC Improv, *1140 Connecticut Ave. NW (p 157)*

Best of the **Bard**
★★ Shakespeare Theatre Company, *610 F St. NW (p 158)*

Best for **Touring Broadway Shows**
★★ National Theatre, *1321 Pennsylvania Ave. NW (p 157)*

Best for **Edgy Playwrights**
★★ Studio Theatre, *1501 14th St. NW, #3 (p 158)*

Best **Outdoor Theater**
★ Wolf Trap Foundation for the Performing Arts, *1645 Trap Rd., Vienna, Virginia (p 158)*

The Woolly Mammoth Theatre Company.

Arts & Entertainment A to Z

★★ Arena Stage SW WATER-FRONT   Artistic Director Molly Smith is known for staging first-rate classical and contemporary productions, attracting leading first men and women from New York and Hollywood. *1101 6th St. SW (at Maine Ave.).* ☎ *202/488-3300. www.arena stage.org. Tickets $25–$75. Metro: Waterfront–SEU.*

★★★ DAR Constitution Hall DOWNTOWN   Everyone from Aretha Franklin to the Smashing Pumpkins has played this popular venue for household-name musicians, comedians, and lecturers. *1776 D St. NW.* ☎ *202/628-4780. www.dar.org. Ticket prices vary. Metro: Farragut West/Farragut North.*

★★ DC Improv DOWNTOWN   Before they were big, Ellen DeGeneres and Dave Chappelle performed at this underground comedy club that still draws top-notch artists weekly from across the country. *1140 Connecticut Ave. NW.* ☎ *202/296-7008. www.dcimprov.com. Tickets are $15–$25. Metro: Farragut North.*

★★ Folger Theatre CAPITOL HILL   Buy tickets here for Shakespearean plays, concerts, and literary readings, as well as fun family activities with a historical twist. *201 E. Capitol St. SE (btw. 2nd and 3rd sts.).* ☎ *202/544-7077. www.folger. edu. Tickets $25–$49. Metro: Capitol South.*

★★ Ford's Theatre DOWNTOWN   This theater, where President Lincoln was shot in 1865 while watching the comedy *Our American Cousin,* is still staging compelling productions today. *511 10th St. NW (btw. E and F sts.).* ☎ *202/347-4833. www.fordstheatre.org. Tickets $25–$55. Metro: Metro Center.*

★★★ Kennedy Center for the Performing Arts FOGGY BOTTOM   Named for the late president, this Washington landmark is both a living memorial and a first-class venue for symphonies, operas, ballets, and touring theatrical and dance productions—not to mention their annual awards. *2700 F St. NW (btw. New Hampshire Ave. and Rock Creek Pkwy.). Box office.* ☎ *202/467-4600. www.kennedy-center.org. Tickets $14–$290. Metro: Foggy Bottom.*

★ Lincoln Theatre U STREET CORRIDOR   Restored to its original splendor, this historic venue has welcomed a host of African-American musicians, from Duke Ellington and Billie Holliday to modern entertainers such as Dick Gregory. *1215 U St. NW (btw. 12th and 13th sts.).* ☎ *202/397-SEAT. Tours: 202/328-6000, ext. 220. www.thelincolntheatre.org. Tickets $20–$200. Metro: Cardozo/U St.*

★★ National Theatre DOWNTOWN   Everyone from Dame Edna to Earth, Wind & Fire plays this

A performance of Henry V *at the Shakespeare Theatre Company.*

historic "theater of Presidents," open since 1835. *1321 Pennsylvania Ave. NW (btw. 13th and 14th sts.).* ☎ *202/628-6161. www.national theatre.org. Tickets $37–$86. Metro: Federal Triangle or Metro Center.*

★★ Shakespeare Theatre Company PENN QUARTER Catch the Bard's best, from *A Midsummer Night's Dream* to *Othello,* in productions with astounding sets and nationally known actors. *610 F St. NW (btw. D and E sts.).* ☎ *202/547-1122. www.shakespearetheatre.org. Tickets $23–$68. Metro: Gallery Place/Chinatown or Archives/Navy Memorial/Penn Quarter.*

★★ Studio Theatre 14TH STREET This theater has earned a stellar reputation for edgy, contemporary productions by playwrights such as Neil LaBute. Its newly renovated space is the crown jewel of the recently revived 14th Street/Logan Circle area. *1501 14th St. NW (at P St.).* ☎ *202/332-3300. www.studio theatre.org. Tickets $32–$62. Metro: Cardozo/U St., Dupont Circle, or McPherson Sq.*

★ Theater J DOWNTOWN This company is nationally and internationally renowned for its progressive Jewish theater programs. *1529 16th St. NW.* ☎ *202/518-9400.*

www.washingtondcjcc.org. Tickets $15–$45. Metro: Dupont Circle.

★★ Warner Theatre CAPITOL HILL This big theater stages a range of performances, from international recording artists (Bob Weir, Hall & Oates) to touring plays (*Golda's Balcony, Cheaters*) to comedic one-man shows (Jim Gaffigan, Lewis Black). *513 13th St. NW (btw. E and F sts.).* ☎ *202/783-4000. www.warner theatredc.com. Ticket prices vary. Metro: Metro Center.*

★ Wolf Trap Foundation for the Performing Arts NORTHERN VIRGINIA Year-round, enjoy touring pop, country, folk, and blues artists, plus dance, theater, opera, and orchestra performances—with outdoor plays and concerts in summer. *1645 Trap Rd. (off Rte. 7), Vienna, Virginia.* ☎ *877/WOLF-TRAP (965-3872). www.wolftrap.org. Tickets $10–$70. No Metro access.*

★★ Woolly Mammoth Theatre Company PENN QUARTER This provocative, experimental company aims to break new ground, showcasing new works by emerging artists. *641 D St. NW (at 7th St.).* ☎ *202/289-2443. www.woollymammoth. net. Tickets $22–$52. Metro: Gallery Place/Chinatown.* ●

A performance at Arena Stage.

D.C. **Hotels**

Previous page: Hotel Helix, in Logan Circle.

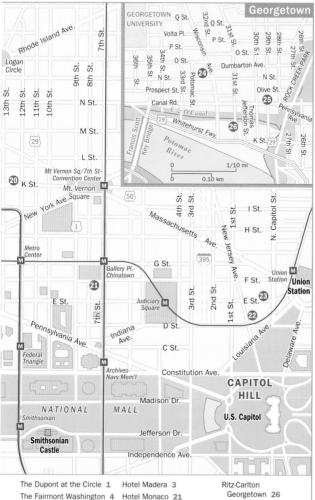

Georgetown

Hotel Best Bets

Where **Activist Hollywood A-Listers Hold Court**
★★ Mandarin Oriental $$$ *1330 Maryland Ave. SW (p 165)*

Where **Hollywood A-Listers Get Some Sleep**
★★ Gold Floor at the Fairmont Washington $$$ *2401 M St. NW (p 163)*

Where Washington's **Young Bucks Mingle**
★★ Hotel George $$ *15 E St. NW (p 163)*

Most Romantic **Bathtub with the Best View**
★★ Willard InterContinental $$$ *1401 Pennsylvania Ave. NW (p 166)*

For Some **Shabby with Your Chic**
★★ Hotel Tabard Inn $$ *1739 N St. NW (p 165)*

Where to **Make a Great Splash**
★★ Washington Plaza Hotel (and its rooftop pool) $$ *10 Thomas Circle NW (p 166)*

Best for **Fashionistas**
★★★ Four Seasons Georgetown $$$$ *2800 Pennsylvania Ave. NW (p 163)*

Best for **Warehouse Luxe**
★★★ Ritz-Carlton Georgetown $$$$ *3100 South St. NW (p 166)*

Where to Meet an **NBA Player**
★★ Hotel Monaco $$ *700 F St. NW (p 164)*

Best for the **Entitled**
★★ The Madison Hotel $$$ *1177 15th St. NW (p 165)*

Best for **Dog Lovers**
★★ Hotel Madera $$ *1310 New Hampshire Ave. NW (p 164)*

Best for **History Buffs**
★★★ Hay-Adams, *1 Lafayette Sq. (p 163)*

Best for **Astrology Fanatics**
★★ Topaz Hotel $$$ *1733 N St. NW (p 166)*

Best for **Fans of All Things Red**
★★ Hotel Rouge $$ *1315 16th St. NW (p 164)*

Best for **Pop Culture Purists** (Who Don't Have Lots of Cash)
★★ Hotel Helix $$ *1430 Rhode Island Ave. NW (p 163)*

A room with a view at the Hay-Adams.

Hotels A to Z

★★★ The Dupont at the Circle
DUPONT CIRCLE   This charming, centrally located inn has six guest rooms, two suites, and one apartment—all with antiques, immaculate bedding, private bathrooms, and Wi-Fi access. *1604 19th St. NW (at Q St. NW).* ☎ *202/332-5251. www.dupontatthecircle.com. 9 units. Doubles from $250. AE, DISC, MC, V. Metro: Dupont Circle.*

★★ The Fairmont Washington
WEST END   Lush atrium gardens set the tone for this elegant, clubby luxury hotel. Its Gold Floor caters to A-listers with free car service, chocolates, and even a pillow menu. *2401 M St. NW (at 24th St. NW).* ☎ *866/540-4505 or 202/429-2400. www.fairmont.com/washington. 415 units. Doubles from $279. AE, DISC, MC, V. Metro: Foggy Bottom.*

★★ kids Four Points Sheraton
PENN QUARTER   In town for a conference at the Convention Center? This clean, safe, and contemporary hotel is ideally located. While its suites are designed for work—with big desks and Internet access—guests can still play in the rooftop pool. *1201 K St. NW (at 12th St. NW).* ☎ *202/289-7600. www.starwoodhotels.com/fourpoints. 265 units. Doubles from $153. AE, DISC, MC, V. Metro: McPherson Square.*

★★★ Four Seasons Georgetown
GEORGETOWN   Travel editors, fashionistas, and movie stars in town to film political thrillers book here for the unparalleled quality and service. The lower-level spa is the capital's best, and M Street shopping is steps away. *2800 Pennsylvania Ave. NW (at M St. NW).* ☎ *202/342-0444. www.fourseasons.com/washington. 211 units. Doubles from $299. AE, DC, DISC, MC, V. Metro: Foggy Bottom.*

★★ kids Georgetown Inn
GEORGETOWN   If you want to be in the heart of Georgetown, this decent (if unspectacular) hotel is the place to stay. Its clubby, dark-wooded interior recently underwent renovations, and the Daily Grill downstairs is family-friendly. *1310 Wisconsin Ave. NW (at N St. NW).* ☎ *888/587-2388 or 202/333-8900. www.georgetowninn.com. 96 units. Doubles from $195–$245. AE, DC, DISC, MC, V. No Metro access. Bus: 30, 32, or 34.*

★★★ Hay-Adams
DOWNTOWN   Steps from the White House, this luxury boutique hotel has great views of Lafayette Park and marries European elegance with a buzzing D.C. insiders' spot, Off the Record Bar. *1 Lafayette Sq. (at 16th and H sts.).* ☎ *202/638-6600. www.hayadams.com. 145 units. Doubles from $199. AE, DC, DISC, MC, V. Metro: Farragut West or McPherson Sq.*

★★ Hotel George
CAPITOL HILL   This modern hotel is minimalist and chic. Hill staffers flock to the hotel bar, at Bistro Bis, and the first president himself welcomes travelers to the capital, in the silk-screen dollar-bill prints that hang in every guest room. *15 E St. NW (at N. Capitol NW).* ☎ *800/546-7866 or 202/347-4200. www.hotelgeorge.com. 139 units. Doubles from $159. AE, DC, DISC, MC, V. Metro: Union Station.*

★★ Hotel Helix
LOGAN CIRCLE   Fans of Andy Warhol, Marilyn Monroe, even PEZ, will adore this boutique hotel with a mission to celebrate all things pop. Interiors are retro, and the funky lounge draws local scene-makers. *1430 Rhode Island Ave. NW (btw. 14th*

A room at the Hotel Helix.

and 15th sts. NW). ☎ 800/706-1202 or 202/462-9001. www.hotelhelix. com. 178 units. Doubles from $149. AE, DC, DISC, MC, V. Metro: Dupont Circle.

★ **Hotel Lombardy** FOGGY BOTTOM   An easy walk from the Mall, this old-time hotel is replete with friendly bellhops, an elevator operator, complimentary shoe shines, and suites that remind you of your grandmother's fanciest guest room—if she were Italian, of course. *2019 Pennsylvania Ave. NW (at I St. NW).* ☎ *202/828-2600. www.hotel lombardy.com. 140 units. Doubles from $109. AE, DC, DISC, MC, V. Metro: Foggy Bottom.*

★★ **Hotel Madera** DUPONT CIRCLE   A boutique hotel for the business traveler: warm-toned yet high-tech guest rooms, with nice touches such as animal-print pillows, a complimentary wine hour, and the option to stow away personal items (such as running shoes) for return guests. Pet friendly, too. *1310 New Hampshire Ave. NW (btw. N and O sts. NW).* ☎ *800/430-1202 or 202/296-7600. www.hotelmadera. com. 82 units. Doubles from $179. AE, DC, DISC, MC, V. Metro: Dupont Circle.*

★★ **Hotel Monaco** PENN QUARTER   Housed in a landmark former post office, this temple to modern cool juxtaposes historic marble and sky-high ceilings with sleek, inviting, vibrantly colored guest rooms. Poste, the swank bar downstairs, attracts visiting NBA stars from the Verizon Center down the block. *700 F St. NW (at 7th St. NW).* ☎ *800/649-1202 or 202/628-7177. www. monaco-dc.com. 183 units. Doubles from $179. AE, DC, DISC, MC, V. Metro: Gallery Place/Chinatown.*

★★ **Hotel Palomar** DUPONT CIRCLE   Art takes center stage at this luxury boutique hotel that offers comfortably appointed rooms with crisp Frette linens and faux lynx throws, plus a stylish restaurant. Pet friendly, too. *2121 P St. NW.* ☎ *877/866-3070 or 202/448-1800. www.hotelpalomar-dc.com. 335 units. Doubles from $149–$359. Metro: Dupont Circle.*

★★ **Hotel Rouge** DUPONT CIRCLE   Young renegades into high-tech hotels will love the red-hot accommodations at this racy boutique inn. Specialty rooms feature flatpanel computer monitors, Sony Wega flatscreen TVs, PlayStation 2, and a video game library. *1315 16th St. NW (btw. Massachusetts Ave. and Scott Circle).* ☎ *800/738-1202*

The lobby at the Hotel Monaco.

The Hotel Rouge lobby.

or 202/232-8000. www.rougehotel.
com. 137 units. Doubles from $179.
AE, DC, DISC, MC, V. Metro: Dupont
Circle.

★★ **Hotel Tabard Inn** DUPONT
CIRCLE   Every room in this eclectic
inn is a romantic mix of original art
and fine early-20th-century
antiques. The excellent restaurant
has a lovely summer garden, cozy
divans, and a fireplace for cold
nights. *1739 N St. NW (btw. 17th and
18th sts.).* ☎ *202/785-1277. www.
tabardinn.com. 40 units. Doubles
with bathroom from $140. AE, DC,
DISC, MC, V. Metro: Dupont Circle or
Farragut North.*

★★★ **The Jefferson Hotel**
DOWNTOWN   Built in 1923, this
stately hotel is just 4 blocks from
the White House. Dine out at its
award-winning restaurant, Plume,
then retire for a nightcap in the
library or to its cozy lounge, Quill.
1200 16th St. NW. ☎ *202/448-2300.
www.jeffersondc.com. 99 units. Doubles from $550. Metro: Farragut
North or Farragut West.*

★★ **The Liaison** CAPITOL HILL
Picky about your pillow? Choose
from six different styles in this
modernly appointed hotel, where
Hill staffers flock to its upscale-
Southern Art and Soul restaurant.

415 New Jersey Ave. NW. ☎ 202/
638-1616. www.affinia.com. 343
units. Doubles from $179–$350.
Metro: Union Station.

★★ **The Madison Hotel** DOWN-
TOWN   Famed for fawning over foreign dignitaries, the Madison is
exactly how you'd imagine a small
Washington hotel to be: traditional,
quiet, well kept, and, yes, dignified.
Spice things up by dining or drinking
at trendy Palette Restaurant downstairs. *1177 15th St. NW (at M St.
NW).* ☎ *800/424-8577 or 202/862-
1600. www.madisonhoteldc.com. 353
units. Doubles from $229. AE, DC,
DISC, MC, V. Metro: Farragut North.*

★★ **Mandarin Oriental** SOUTH-
WEST   A feng shui expert designed
the rooms here—some with spectacular views of the Southwest
Marina and the Jefferson Memorial.
Eastern luxury meets Western luxury in the beautifully balanced silk
wall coverings, bamboo embellishments, and marble bathrooms. *1330
Maryland Ave. SW (at 12th St. SW).*
☎ *888/888-1778 or 202/554-8588.
www.mandarinoriental.com. 400
units. Doubles from $255. AE, DC,
DISC, MC, V. Metro: Smithsonian.*

★★ **The Mayflower Hotel**
DOWNTOWN   The quintessential
grande dame of Washington, this

historic hotel with a marble interior lobby and well-appointed rooms is still comfortable enough to make you feel right at home. *1127 Connecticut Ave. NW.* ☎ *202/347-3000. 583 units and 74 suites. Doubles from $250. AE, DISC, MC, V. Metro: Farragut North.*

★★★ Ritz-Carlton Georgetown

GEORGETOWN   Historic architecture meets modern elegance in this upscale hotel, once the site of a 19th-century brick-and-steel incinerator. If the guest rooms' marble bathrooms and goose-down pillows don't soothe your soul, book a treatment at the pampering spa. *3100 South St. NW (at 31st St. NW).* ☎ *800/542-8680 or 202/912-4100. www.ritzcarlton.com/hotels/george town. 86 units. Doubles from $349. AE, DC, DISC, MC, V. No Metro access (see box, p 91).*

★ kids The River Inn FOGGY BOTTOM

If you love to travel but hate to blow so much cash dining out, book at this centrally located, modern boutique hotel; each spacious guest room has a full kitchenette. *924 25th St. NW (at K St. NW).* ☎ *888/874-0100. www.theriverinn. com. 126 units. Doubles from $99. AE, DC, DISC, MC, V. Metro: Foggy Bottom.*

★★★ St. Regis Hotel DOWNTOWN

This stately hotel a mere few blocks from the White House recently underwent a massive makeover to restore it to its original 1926 glamour. *923 16th and K sts. NW.* ☎ *202/638-2626. www.stregis. com. 175 units. Doubles from $190–$460. Metro: Farragut North.*

★★ Topaz Hotel DUPONT

CIRCLE   This ambient palace offers free tarot card readings, horoscopes, exotic interior textures, and healing in-room spa services. *1733 N St. NW (btw. 17th and 18th sts.).* ☎ *202/393-3000. www. topazhotel.com. 99 units. Doubles from $199. AE, DC, DISC, MC, V. Metro: Dupont Circle or Farragut North.*

★ W Hotel DOWNTOWN   Just

blocks from the White House and National Mall, this swank hotel offers all of the modern and efficient services you'll need with a prime location in the center of D.C. Its POV Rooftop Bar offers spectacular views of the city below. *515 15th St. NW.* ☎ *202/661-2400. www. wwashingtondc.com. 317 units. Doubles from $329. AE, DISC, MC, V. Metro: Metro Center.*

★★ Washington Plaza Hotel

LOGAN CIRCLE   Rich and famous hipsters who might otherwise be in Miami flock here for the exclusive outdoor pool and buzzing scene at the International Bar. *10 Thomas Circle NW (at 14th St. NW).* ☎ *800/ 424-1140 or 202/842-1300. www. washingtonplazahotel.com. 340 units. Doubles from $189. AE, DC, DISC, MC, V. Metro: McPherson Sq.*

★★ Willard InterContinental

Hotel DOWNTOWN   Beaux-Arts architecture meets history here—where Martin Luther King, Jr. wrote his "I Have a Dream" speech, and every president from Grant to "W" has bunked at least once for the night. Ask about the romantic tub in the honeymoon suite. *1401 Pennsylvania Ave. NW (at 14th St. NW).* ☎ *800/487-2537 or 202/628-9100. www.washington.intercontinental. com. 341 units. Doubles from $239. AE, DC, DISC, MC, V. Metro: Metro Center.* ●

The
Savvy Traveler

Before You Go

Government Tourist Offices
Destination DC (901 7th St. NW, Washington, DC 20001-3719 (☎ 800/422-8644 or 202/789-7000; www.washington.org) details hotels, restaurants, attractions, shops, and more.

Also take a look at the D.C. government's website, www.dc.gov, and www.culturaltourismdc.org for more information about the city.

For additional information about Washington's most popular tourist spots, visit the National Park Service website, www.nps.gov/nacc, and the Smithsonian Institution's site, www.si.edu.

The Best Times to Go
The city's peak seasons generally coincide with the sessions of Congress and springtime. When Congress is "in," from about the second week in September until Thanksgiving, and again from about mid-January

through June, hotels are full with guests on business.

Mid-March through June traditionally is the most frenzied season, when families and school groups descend to see the cherry blossoms. It's also a popular season for protest marches.

To avoid crowds, consider visiting at the end of August and early September or between Thanksgiving and mid-January; though the lighting of the National Christmas Tree is very popular.

The July 4th Independence Day celebration is spectacular, but the weather is very hot and humid in July and August. Many of Washington's performance stages close, although some outdoor arenas and parks host events.

For event schedules, see www.washington.org, www.culturaltourismdc.org, www.dc.gov, and www.washingtonpost.com.

Useful Numbers & Websites

- **National Park Service** (☎ 202/619-7222; www.nps.gov/ncro). You'll reach a real person and not a recording when you phone this number with questions about the monuments, the Mall, national park lands, and events taking place at these locations.

- **Dial-A-Park** (☎ 202/619-7275). This is a recording of information about Park Service events and attractions.

- **Dial-A-Museum** (☎ 202/633-1000; www.si.edu). This recording offers the locations of the 16

Washington Smithsonian museums and their daily activities.

- The **Washington, D.C. Visitor Information Center** (☎ 866/324-7386; www.itcdc.com) is a small visitor center in the immense Ronald Reagan International Trade Center Building (1300 Pennsylvania Ave. NW).

- The **Smithsonian Information Center,** in the "Castle," 1000 Jefferson Dr. SW (☎ 202/633-1000; www.si.edu), is open every day (except Christmas) from 9am to 5pm Monday through Friday and 9am to 4pm Saturday through Sunday.

Previous page: The D.C. Metro.

AVERAGE TEMPERATURES & RAINFALL IN WASHINGTON, D.C.

	JAN	FEB	MAR	APR	MAY	JUNE
Avg. High (°F/°C)	44/7	46/8	54/12	66/19	76/25	83/29
Avg. Low (°F/°C)	30/-1	29/-1	36/2	46/8	56/14	65/19
Rainfall (in.)	3.21	2.63	3.6	2.71	3.82	3.13

	JULY	AUG	SEPT	OCT	NOV	DEC
Avg. High (°F/°C)	87/31	85/30	79/26	68/20	57/14	46/8
Avg. Low (°F/°C)	69/20	68/20	61/16	50/10	39/4	32/0
Rainfall (in.)	3.66	3.44	3.79	3.22	3.03	3.05

- The **American Automobile Association (AAA)** has a large central office near the White House, at 1405 G St. NW, between G Street and New York Avenue NW, Washington, DC 20005-2111 (☎ 202/481-6811).

Getting **There**

By Plane

Domestic airlines with scheduled flights into all three of Washington, D.C.'s airports, Washington Dulles International **(Dulles)**, Ronald Reagan Washington National **(National)**, and Baltimore–Washington International **(BWI)**, include **American** (☎ 800/433-7300; www.aa.com), **Delta** (☎ 800/221-1212; www.delta.com), **United** (☎ 800/864-8331; www.united.com), and **US Airways** (☎ 800/428-4322; www.usairways.com).

Quite a few low-fare airlines serve all three D.C. airports. **Southwest Airlines** (☎ 800/435-9792; www.southwest.com), at **BWI Airport,** has 162 daily flights to more than 35 cities. Another bargain airline at National, BWI and Dulles is **AirTran** (☎ 800/247-8726; www.airtran.com).

Discount airlines that serve **Dulles** are **Virgin Atlantic** (☎ 800/862-8621; www.virginatlantic.com), **AirTran, Southwest,** and **JetBlue** (☎ 800/538-2583; www.jetblue.com).

Four discount airlines fly into **National Airport: AirTran, Jet-Blue, Frontier** (☎ 800/432-1359; www.frontierairlines.com) and **Spirit** (☎ 800/772-7177; www.spirit air.com).

Shuttle Service from New York, Boston & Chicago

Delta and US Airways continue to dominate the D.C.–East Coast shuttle service. Between the two of them, hourly or almost-hourly shuttle service runs between Boston's Logan Airport and Washington, and New York's La Guardia Airport and Washington. The **Delta Shuttle** (☎ 800/933-5935) travels daily between New York and Washington, while the **US Airways Shuttle** (☎ 800/428-4322) operates daily between Boston and Washington and New York and Washington. **Southwest** (see details above) offers nearly hourly service daily between BWI and Chicago's Midway Airport, Providence, Hartford, Long Island, Manchester (New Hampshire), Orlando, and Nashville.

Getting into Town from the Airport

All three airports offer the following options for getting into the city.

TAXI SERVICE   For a trip downtown, expect a taxi to cost anywhere from $10 to $20 for the 10- to 15-minute ride from National Airport (dependent on time of day and number of passengers and luggage); $55 to $65 for the 30- to 40-minute ride from Dulles Airport; and $55 to $65 for the 45-minute ride from BWI (depending on the time of day, number of passengers, and amount of luggage).

SUPERSHUTTLE   Vans (☎ 800/258-3826; www.supershuttle.com) offer shared-ride, door-to-door service. You can't reserve space on the van for a ride from the airport, so you'll likely have to wait 15 to 30 minutes to board and then make other stops before reaching your destination. If you arrive after midnight, call the 24-hour toll-free number above from National Airport or ☎ 703/416-7884 from both Dulles and BWI. To reach downtown, expect to pay about $14, plus $10 for each additional person from National; $29, plus $10 per additional person from Dulles; and $35 to $40, plus $12 per additional person from BWI. If you're calling SuperShuttle for a ride from D.C. to an airport, reserve at least 24 hours in advance.

LIMOUSINES   Prices start at $25 at National, $42 at Dulles, and $95 at BWI, for private car transportation downtown. For pickup from BWI, reserve passage by calling ☎ 800/410-4444; for pickup from National or Dulles, try **Red Top Executive Sedan** (☎ 703/522-3300) or consult the Yellow Pages.

Free hotel/motel shuttles operate from all three airports to certain nearby properties. Ask about such transportation when you book a room at your hotel.

Individual transportation options at each airport are as follows:

FROM RONALD REAGAN WASHINGTON NATIONAL AIRPORT   **Metrorail's** (☎ 202/637-7000) Yellow and Blue lines stop at the airport and connect via an enclosed walkway to level two, the concourse level, of the main terminal, adjacent to terminals B and C. The ride downtown takes 15 to 20 minutes (longer at rush hour). It is safe, convenient, and cheap, from $1.60 and up (fares increase during rush hours).

Metrobuses (☎ 202/637-7000) also serve the area, should you be going somewhere off the Metro route, but Metrorail is faster.

If you're renting a car from on-site **car-rental** agencies **Alamo** (☎ 703/414-8300), **Budget** (☎ 703/872-0320), **Dollar** (☎ 866/434-2226), **Hertz** (☎ 703/419-6300), **National** (☎ 703/414-8300) or **Thrifty** (☎ 877/283-0898), go to level two, the concourse level, follow the pedestrian walkway to the parking garage, find garage A, and descend one flight. You can also take the free Airport Shuttle (look for the sign on the curb outside the terminal) to parking garage A. If you've rented from off-premises agencies such as **Enterprise** (☎ 703/414-8310), head outside the baggage claim area of your terminal, and catch the shuttle bus marked for your agency.

To get downtown by car, follow the signs for the George Washington Parkway. Then take I-395 North to Washington. Take the I-395 North exit, which takes you across the 14th Street Bridge. Stay in the left lane crossing the bridge and follow the signs for Route 1, which will put you on 14th Street NW. Ask your hotel for directions from 14th Street and Constitution Avenue NW.

A more scenic route runs to the left of the GW Parkway as you follow the signs for Memorial Bridge. You'll be driving alongside the Potomac River, with the monuments in view; as you cross over Memorial Bridge, the Lincoln Memorial greets you. Stay left coming over the bridge, swoop around left of the Memorial, turn left on 23rd Street NW, right on Constitution Avenue, and then left again on 15th Street NW (the Washington Monument will be to your right), into the heart of downtown.

FROM WASHINGTON DULLES INTERNATIONAL AIRPORT   The **Washington Flyer Express Bus** runs between Dulles and the West Falls Church Metro station, where you can board a train for D.C. In the airport, look for signs for the "Dulles Airport Shuttle." Buses to the West Falls Church Metro station run daily, every 30 minutes, and cost $10 one-way.

More convenient is the **Metrobus** that runs between Dulles and the L'Enfant Plaza Metro station, within walking distance of the National Mall and Smithsonian museums. The bus departs hourly, costs only $3, and takes 45 to 60 minutes. SmartTrip card riders (see below) are eligible for a discount.

For rental car pick-up at Dulles, head down the ramp near your baggage claim area, and walk outside to the curb to look for your rental car's shuttle bus stop. The buses come by every 5 minutes or so en route to nearby rental lots. These include **Alamo** (☎ 703/661-3230), **Avis** (☎ 703/661-3500), **Budget** (☎ 703/437-9559), **Dollar** (☎ 703/661-6924), **Hertz** (☎ 703/471-6020) **Enterprise** (☎ 703/661-8800), **National** (☎ 703/661-3200), and **Thrifty** (☎ 877/283-0898).

To reach downtown from Dulles by car, exit the airport and stay on the Dulles Access Road, which leads right into I-66 East. Follow I-66 East, which takes you across the Theodore Roosevelt Memorial Bridge. Be sure to stay in the center lane as you cross the bridge; this will put

you on Constitution Avenue. Ask your hotel for directions from this point.

FROM BALTIMORE–WASHINGTON INTERNATIONAL AIRPORT   Washington's Metro service runs an Express Metro Bus ("B30") between its Metrorail Green Line Greenbelt station and BWI Airport. In the airport, head to the lower level and look for signs to find the bus, which runs daily every 40 minutes, takes about 30 minutes, and costs $3. At the Greenbelt Metro station, you purchase a Metro fare card and board a Metro train, which will take you into the city. Depending on where you want to go, you can either stay on the Green Line train to your designated stop or get off at the Fort Totten Station to transfer to a Red Line train, which stops include Union Station (near Capitol Hill) and various downtown locations.

Amtrak (☎ 800/872-7245) and **Maryland Rural Commuter (MARC;** ☎ 866/743-3682) trains also run into the city. Both travel between the BWI Railway Station (☎ 410/672-6169) and Washington's Union Station (☎ 202/906-3104), about a 30-minute ride. Amtrak's service is daily (ticket prices range from $13–$38 per person, one-way, depending on time and train type), while MARC's is weekdays only ($6 per person, one-way). A courtesy shuttle runs every 10 minutes or so between the airport and the train station; stop at the desk near the baggage-claim area to check for train or bus departure times. Trains depart about every hour.

BWI operates a large, off-site, car-rental facility. From the ground transportation area, a shuttle bus transports you to the lot. Rental agencies include **Avis** (☎ 410/859-1680), **Alamo** (☎ 410/859-8092), **Budget** (☎ 410/691-2913), **Dollar**

(☎ 410/850-7112), **Enterprise** (☎ 800/325-8007, **Hertz** (☎ 410/850-7400), **National** (☎ 410/859-8860), and **Thrifty** (☎ 410/850-7112).

To reach Washington: Look for signs for I-195 and follow I-195 West until you see signs for Washington and the Baltimore-Washington Parkway (I-295); head south on I-295. Get off I-295 when you see the signs for Route 50/New York Avenue, which leads into the District, via New York Avenue. Ask your hotel for specific directions from New York Avenue NE.

By Car

If you are like most visitors to Washington, you're planning to drive here via one of the following major highways: I-270, I-95, and I-295 from the north; I-95 and I-395, Route 1, and Route 301 from the south; Route 50/301 and Route 450 from the east; and Route 7, Route 50, I-66, and Route 29/211 from the west.

No matter which road you take, you will likely have to navigate part of the **Capital Beltway** (I-495 and I-95). The Beltway girds the city, about 66 miles (106km) around, with more than 56 interchanges or exits, and is nearly always congested, especially during weekday morning and evening rush hours (roughly 6–9:30am and 3–7pm). Commuter traffic on the Beltway rivals or surpasses that of L.A.'s major freeways, and drivers can get crazy, weaving in and out of traffic.

By Train

Amtrak (☎ 800/USA-RAIL [872-7245]; www.amtrak.com) offers daily service to Washington from New York, Boston, Chicago, and Los Angeles (you change trains in Chicago). Amtrak also travels daily from points south of Washington, including Raleigh, Charlotte, Atlanta, cities in Florida, and New Orleans.

Metroliner service—which costs a little more but provides faster transit and roomier, more comfortable seating than regular trains—is available between New York and Washington, D.C. and points in between. Even faster, roomier, and more expensive are Amtrak's high-speed **Acela Express** trains. The trains travel 150 mph (241kmph), linking Boston, New York, and Washington.

Acela Express trains travel between New York and Washington in 2 hours and 50 minutes (about 20 min. faster than the Metroliner), and between Boston and Washington in about 6½ hours.

Amtrak trains arrive at historic **Union Station,** 2 Massachusetts Ave. NE (☎ 202/289-1908; www.unionstationdc.com).

By Bus

Coming from New York? **Bolt Bus** (www.boltbus.com) provides daily express service from Manhattan to Washington, and vice versa. Its buses are new and outfitted with free wireless access and plug-ins for charging laptops and cell phones. The Bolt Bus picks up and drops off in a prime downtown location too, at H Street between 9th and 10th streets. (A red Bolt Bus sign marks the spot.) Fares can run up to $20.

A comparable alternative to Bolt Bus, **Megabus** (www.megabus.com; ☎ 877/462-6342) travels many times a day between Washington, D.C.'s Union Station and NYC, as well as 17 other locations, including Boston, Toronto, and Knoxville, Tennessee. Fares are as low as $1 one-way, depending on distance and other factors; most fares run in the $13 to $25 range.

Another option is the well-known **Chinatown Bus** (www.chinatown-bus.com) that makes frequent runs between New York and Washington. Its buses are older and can be crowded, though. Fares range from $1 to $20.

Vamoose (☎ 301/718-0036; www.vamoosebus.com) offers service for $30 each way from New York City (near Penn Station) to Bethesda, Maryland, and Arlington, Virginia, where you can make a connection to D.C.'s Metro system.

Getting **Around**

By Metro

Metrorail's (www.wmata.com) system of 86 stations and 106 miles (171km) of track includes stops near most sightseeing attractions and extends to suburban Maryland and northern Virginia. Five lines—Red, Blue, Orange, Yellow, and Green—connect at several points, making transfers easy. All but Yellow and Green Line trains stop at Metro Center; all but Red Line trains stop at L'Enfant Plaza; all but Blue and Orange Line trains stop at Gallery Place/Chinatown.

Metro stations are identified by brown columns bearing the station's name topped by the letter *f* . Below the *f* is a colored stripe or stripes indicating the line or lines that stop there. The free *Metro System Pocket Guide* has a map and lists the closest Metro stops to points of interest. You can download a copy from the website, www.wmata.com.

To enter or exit a Metro station, you need a computerized **fare card,** available at vending machines near the entrance. The machines take credit cards or nickels, dimes, quarters, and bills from $1 to $20; they can return up to $4.95 in change (coins only). At this time, the minimum fare to enter the system is $1.70, which pays for rides to and from any point within 7 miles (11km) of boarding during nonpeak hours; during peak hours (Mon–Fri 5–9:30am and 3–7pm), $2.10 takes you only 3 miles (5km). The maximum you will pay to the farthest destination is $5.75. Be forewarned that Metro Authority is always contemplating a fare hike, so these prices may change.

If you plan to take several Metrorail trips during your stay, put more value on the fare card to avoid having to purchase a new card each time you ride. For stays of more than a few days, your best value is the **7-Day Fast Pass,** $47 per person for unlimited travel; **1-Day Rail Passes,** $9 per person for unlimited passage that day, after 9:30am weekdays, and all day on Saturday, Sunday, and holidays, are a good option if you'll be riding the Metro many times in one day. You can buy these passes online or use the passes/fare cards machine in the station.

Metrorail opens at 5am weekdays and 7am Saturday and Sunday, operating until midnight Sunday through Thursday, and until 3am Friday and Saturday. Call ☎ 202/637-7000, or visit www.wmata.com, for holiday hours and information on Metro routes.

By Bus

The **Metrobus** system operates 12,435 stops on its 1,489-square-mile (3,856-sq.-km) route, extending into the Virginia and Maryland suburbs. Stops have red, white, and blue signs that tell you what buses pull into a stop, but not where they go. *Warning:* Don't rely on the bus schedules posted at bus stops—they're often out of date. For more information, call ☎ 202/637-7000.

The Savvy Traveler

Base fare in the District is $1.70 for those using cash, and $1.50 if you use a SmarTrip; transfers are free and valid for 2 hours from boarding. If you'll be in Washington for a while and plan to use the buses a lot, consider a 1-week pass ($15), available online and at the Metro Center station and other outlets. Buy tokens at the Metro Center Sales Office, at 12th and F streets, the 12th Street entrance.

Most buses operate daily almost around the clock. Service is frequent on weekdays, especially during peak hours. On weekends and late at night, service is less frequent.

Up to two children 4 and under ride free with a paying passenger on Metrobus. **Reduced fares** are available for seniors (☎ 202/637-7000) and people with disabilities (☎ 202/962-1100). If you leave something on a bus, a train, or in a station, call Lost and Found at ☎ 202/962-1195.

By Car
More than half of all visitors arrive by car. Once you get here, though, my advice is to park it and walk or use the Metrorail. Traffic is always thick during the week, parking spots are scarce, and parking lots are pricey.

Watch out for **traffic circles.** Cars in the circle have the right of way, but no one heeds this rule. Cars zoom in without a glance at the cars already there.

Sections of certain streets become **one-way** at rush hour: Rock Creek Parkway, Canal Road, and 17th Street NW are three examples. Other streets during rush hour change the direction of some of their traffic lanes: Connecticut Avenue NW is the main one. Lit-up traffic signs alert you as to what's going on, but pay attention. You can make a right on a red light, unless a sign is posted prohibiting it.

Car Rentals/Shares
All the major car-rental companies are represented here. See area airports at the beginning of this chapter for phone numbers for each company's airport locations. Within the District, car-rental locations include **Avis,** 1722 M St. NW (☎ 202/467-6585) and 4400 Connecticut Ave. NW (☎ 202/686-5149); **Budget,** 1722 M St. NW (☎ 202/457-1916); **Enterprise,** 2660 Woodley Rd. NW (☎ 202/232-4443); **Hertz,** Union Station (☎ 202/289-5366); **Alamo,** Union Station (☎ 888/826-6893).

Whether you need a car for an hour or a month, **Zipcar** (☎ 866/494-7227 or 202/737-4900; www.zipcar.com) offers its "members"—anyone can join for $60—flexible car-use arrangements, with gas, insurance, and other services included. Zipcar charges $8 an hour; its daily rate is $83.

The latest car share service to arrive in D.C. is **Car2Go** (☎ 877/488-4224; www.car2go.com) which offers fun blue-and-white SmartCars to zip around the city. "Members" can reserve a car by the minute ($0.38), hour ($13.99) or day ($72.99). Every mile over 150 miles will be charged at 45 cents per mile.

Given that hotels charge about $26 for overnight parking, the Zipcar and Car2Go deals, which include parking and fuel, could still be cost-effective.

Travelers with Limited Mobility
Washington, D.C. is one of the most accessible cities in the world for travelers with limited mobility. The best overall source for information about accessibility at specific Washington hotels, restaurants, shopping malls, and attractions is the non-profit organization **Access Information.** You can read their information

(including restaurant reviews) online at www.disabilityguide.org.

The **Washington Metropolitan Transit Authority** publishes accessibility information on its website www.wmata.com, or you can call ☎ 301/562-5360 with questions about Metro services for travelers with disabilities, including how to obtain an ID card that entitles you to discounted fares. (Make sure that you call at least 3 weeks ahead to allow enough time to obtain an ID card.) For up-to-date information about how Metro is running the day you're using it, call ☎ 202/637-7000.

Each station has an elevator with Braille number plates and wide fare gates for wheelchair users; rail cars are fully accessible. Metro has installed punctuated rubber tiles to warn visually impaired riders that they're nearing the tracks; barriers between rail cars prevent the blind from mistaking the gap for entry to a car. For the hearing impaired, flashing lights indicate arriving trains; for the visually impaired,

door chimes let you know when doors are closing. Train operators make station and onboard announcements of train destinations and stops. Nearly all Metrobuses have wheelchair lifts and kneeling devices at the curb. The TTY number for Metro information is ☎ 202/638-3780.

Major Washington museums, including all **Smithsonian museum buildings,** are accessible to wheelchair visitors. A comprehensive free publication called **Smithsonian Access** lists all services available to visitors with mobility issues. Call ☎ 202/633-2921 or TTY 202/633-4353, or find the information online at www.si.edu/Visit/VisitorsWith Disabilities.

Likewise, theaters and all of the memorials are equipped to accommodate visitors with disabilities. There's limited parking for visitors with disabilities at some of these locations. Call ahead for accessibility information and special services.

Fast **Facts**

AREA CODES In the District of Columbia, it's ☎ **202;** in suburban Virginia, ☎ **703;** in suburban Maryland, ☎ **301.** You must use the area code when dialing any number, even for local calls within the District or to nearby Maryland or Virginia suburbs.

ATMS **Automated teller machines (ATMs)** are on almost every block. Most accept Visa, MasterCard, American Express, and ATM cards from other U.S. banks. Expect to pay up to $3 per transaction if you're not using your own bank's ATM.

BUSINESS HOURS Offices are usually open weekdays from 9am to

5pm. Banks are open Monday through Thursday from 9am to 3pm, 9am to 5pm on Friday, and sometimes Saturday mornings. Stores typically open between 9 and 10am and close between 5 and 6pm from Monday through Saturday. Stores in shopping complexes or malls tend to stay open late: until about 9pm on weekdays and weekends, and many malls and larger department stores are open on Sunday.

CAR RENTALS See "Getting Around," earlier in this chapter.

DRUGSTORES **CVS,** Washington's major drugstore chain (with more than 40 stores), has two convenient 24-hour locations: in the West End, at 2000 M St. NW (☎ 202/862-8417), and at Dupont Circle (☎ 202/785-1466), which features a round-the-clock pharmacy. Check your phone book for other convenient locations.

ELECTRICITY   Like Canada, the United States uses 110–120 volts AC (60 cycles), compared to 220–240 volts AC (50 cycles) in most of Europe, Australia, and New Zealand. If your small appliances use 220–240 volts, you'll need a 110-volt transformer and a plug adapter with two flat parallel pins to operate them here. Downward converters that change 220–240 volts to 110–120 volts are difficult to find in the United States, so bring one with you.

EMBASSIES & CONSULATES   All embassies are in D.C., the nation's capital. Online, you will find a complete listing, with links to each embassy, at www.embassy.org/embassies/index.html.

Here are the addresses of several: **Australia,** 1601 Massachusetts Ave. NW (☎ 202/797-3000; www.usa.embassy.gov.au; **Canada,** 501 Pennsylvania Ave. NW (☎ 202/682-1740; www.canadianembassy.org); **Ireland,** 2234 Massachusetts Ave. NW (☎ 202/462-3939; www.embassyofireland.org); **New Zealand,** 37 Observatory Circle NW (☎ 202/328-4800; www.nzembassy.org); and the **United Kingdom,** 3100 Massachusetts Ave. NW (☎ 202/588-6500; http://ukinusa.fco.gov.uk/en.

EMERGENCIES   In any emergency, call ☎ **911.**

HOLIDAYS   Banks, government offices, post offices, and many stores, restaurants, and museums are closed on the following legal national holidays: January 1 (New Year's Day), the third Monday in January (Martin Luther King, Jr. Day), January 20 (Inauguration Day), the third Monday in February (Presidents' Day, Washington's Birthday), the last Monday in May (Memorial Day), July 4 (Independence Day), the first Monday in September (Labor Day), the second Monday in October (Columbus Day), November 11 (Veterans Day/Armistice Day), the fourth Thursday in November (Thanksgiving Day), and December 25 (Christmas).

HOSPITALS   If you don't require immediate ambulance transportation but still need emergency-room treatment, call one of the following hospitals (and get directions): **Children's Hospital National Medical Center,** 111 Michigan Ave. NW (☎ 202/476-5005); **George Washington University Hospital,** 900 23rd St. NW at Washington Circle (☎ 202/715-4000); **Georgetown University Medical Center,** 3800 Reservoir Rd. NW (☎ 202/444-2000); or **Howard University Hospital,** 2041 Georgia Ave. NW (☎ 202/865-6100).

INTERNET ACCESS   Your hotel is your best bet since many hotels now offer free Internet access. **Kramerbooks & Afterwords Café,** 1517 Connecticut Ave. NW (☎ 202/387-1400) in Dupont Circle has one computer available for free Internet access (15-min. limit). **Tryst,** 2459 18th St., NW (☎ 202/232-5500) is also a good stop for free wireless access. Most **Starbucks, Caribou Coffees,** and **Cosi** coffee shops also offer free Internet access.

LIQUOR LAWS   The legal age for purchase and consumption of alcoholic beverages is 21; proof of age is required, so bring an ID when you go out. Liquor stores are closed on Sunday. Gourmet grocery stores, mom-and-pop grocery stores, and 7-Eleven convenience stores often sell beer and wine, even on Sunday.

Do not carry open containers of alcohol in your car or any public area that isn't zoned for alcohol consumption. The police can fine you on the spot. And nothing will ruin your trip faster than getting a citation for DUI (driving under the influence), so don't even think about driving while intoxicated.

MAIL The main post office in the capital is the **National Capitol Station,** 2 Massachusetts Ave. NE (☎ 202/523-2368; www.usps.com). Mailboxes are blue with a red-and-white stripe and carry the inscription fiE‹E7 x¢ All U.S. addresses have a five-digit postal code (or zip code), after the two-letter state abbreviation. This code is essential for prompt delivery.

At press time, domestic postage rates were 28¢ for a postcard and 44¢ for a letter. For international mail, a first-class letter of up to 1 ounce costs 98¢ (75¢ to Canada and 79¢ to Mexico), a first-class postcard costs 98¢ (75¢ to Canada and 79¢ to Mexico), and a preprinted postal aerogramme costs 75¢.

NEWSPAPERS & MAGAZINES At the airport, pick up a free copy of *Washington Flyer* magazine (www.washingtonflyer.com), which is handy as a planning tool.

Washington has two daily newspapers: the *Washington Post* (www.washingtonpost.com) and the *Washington Times* (www.washingtontimes.com). The Friday "Weekend" section of the *Post* is essential for finding out what's going on, recreation-wise. *City Paper,* published every Thursday and available free at downtown shops and restaurants, covers some of the same material but is a better guide to the club and art-gallery scene.

Also on newsstands is *Washingtonian,* a monthly magazine with features, often about the "100 Best" this or that (doctors, restaurants, and so on) in Washington; the magazine also offers a calendar of events, restaurant reviews, and profiles of Washingtonians.

POLICE In an emergency, dial ☎ **911.** For a nonemergency, call ☎ **311.**

SAFETY Washington, like any urban area, has a criminal element, so it's important to stay alert and take normal safety precautions.

Ask your hotel front-desk staff or the city's tourist office if you're in doubt about which neighborhoods are safe.

SMOKING In 2006, D.C. lawmakers banned smoking in bars, restaurants, and public places, with exemptions for outdoor areas, hotel rooms, retail tobacco outlets, and cigar bars.

TAXES The U.S. has no value-added tax (VAT) or other indirect tax at the national level. The sales tax on merchandise is 6% in D.C. The tax on restaurant meals is 10%, and you'll pay 14% hotel tax. The hotel tax in Maryland varies by county from 5% to 8%. The hotel tax in Virginia also varies by county, averaging about 9.75%.

TELEPHONE & FAX Private corporations run the telephone system in the U.S., so rates—especially for long-distance service and operator-assisted calls—can vary widely.

Many convenience groceries and packaging services sell **prepaid calling cards** in denominations up to $50; these can be the least expensive way to call home. Many public phones at airports now accept American Express, MasterCard, and Visa credit cards. **Local calls** made from public pay phones (if you can find one) in most locales cost either 25¢ or 35¢. Pay phones do not accept pennies, and few will take anything larger than a quarter. You may want to look into leasing a cellphone for the duration of your trip.

Most long-distance and international calls can be placed directly from any phone. **For calls within the United States and to Canada,** dial 1 followed by the area code and the seven-digit number. **For other**

international calls, dial 011 followed by the country code, city code, and the telephone number of the person you are calling.

Calls to area codes **800, 888, 877,** and **866** are toll-free. However, calls to numbers in area codes **700** and **900** (chat lines, bulletin boards, "dating" services, and so on) can be very expensive—usually a charge of 95¢ to $3 or more per minute, and they sometimes have minimum charges that can run as high as $15 or more.

For **reversed-charge or collect calls,** and for person-to-person calls, dial 0 (zero, not the letter ¤) followed by the area code and number you want; an operator will then come on the line to assist you. If you're calling abroad, ask for the overseas operator.

For **local directory assistance (information),** dial ☎ 411; for long-distance information, dial ☎ 1, then the appropriate area code and 555-1212.

TIME   Washington, D.C. observes Eastern Standard Time (EST), like New York City. **Daylight saving time** is in effect from early March through early November. Daylight saving time moves the clock 1 hour ahead of standard time. At 1am on the last Sunday in October, clocks are set back 1 hour. For the correct time, call the U.S. Naval Observatory Master Clock at ☎ 202/762-1401.

TIPPING   In hotels, tip **bellhops** at least $1 per bag, and tip the

chamber staff $1 to $2 per day. Tip the **doorman** or **concierge** only if he or she has provided you with some specific service (for example, calling a cab for you or obtaining difficult-to-get theater tickets). Tip the **valet-parking attendant** $1 every time you get your car.

In restaurants, bars, and nightclubs, tip **service staff** 15% to 20% of the check, tip **bartenders** 10% to 15%, tip **checkroom attendants** $1 per garment, and tip **valet-parking attendants** $1 per vehicle. Tipping is not expected in cafeterias and fast-food restaurants.

Tip **cabdrivers** 15% of the fare.

As for other service personnel, tip **skycaps** at airports at least $1 per bag, and tip **hairdressers** and **barbers** 15% to 20%.

Tipping ushers at movies and theaters, and gas-station attendants, is not expected.

TOILETS   You won't find public toilets or restrooms on the streets in D.C., but they can be found in hotel lobbies, bars, restaurants, coffee shops, museums, department stores, railway and bus stations, and service stations. Large hotels and fast-food restaurants are probably the best bet for good, clean facilities. Restaurants and bars in heavily visited areas may reserve their restrooms for patrons; purchasing a cup of coffee or soft drink will usually qualify you as a customer.

WEATHER   Visit www.weather.com. Also see the chart on p 169.

Recommended **Reading**

Fiction lovers might pick up books by Ward Just, including his collection of stories *The Congressman Who Loved Flaubert;* Ann Berne's *A Crime in the Neighborhood;* Marita Golden's *The Edge of Heaven;* or Allen

Drury's *Advise and Consent.* Or consider a mystery in which the plot revolves around the capital, such as Margaret Truman's series that includes *Murder at the Smithsonian, Murder at the Kennedy Center,* and so on, or George Pelecanos's hard-core thrillers that take you to parts of Washington you'll never see as a tourist, such as in *Hell to Pay*, *Drama City*, and, in 2009, *The Way Home*; he also recently compiled and edited *D.C. Noir*, a collection of 16 gritty short stories, including one by Pelecanos himself.

National Book Award finalist *Lost in the City*—by Pulitzer Prize–winning novelist Edward P. Jones—is a beautifully written collection of short stories about the daily lives of African Americans in the capital.

Contenders, by Terence Winch, is a lively collection of stories about life in Washington in the 1970s and 1980s, as lived by the young and restless of that time.

History buffs shouldn't miss Arthur Schlesinger's *The Birth of the Nation*; F. Cary's *Urban Odyssey*; or David Brinkley's *Washington at War*. Paul Dickson's *On This Spot* traces the history of the city by revealing exactly what took place at specific locations—"on this spot"—in years gone by, neighborhood by neighborhood.

If you like your history leavened with humor, purchase Christopher Buckley's *Washington Schlepped Here: Walking in the Nation's Capital*, an irreverent nonfiction take on D.C.'s famous sites and characters.

Buckley has also written a couple of funny, Washington-based novels, *The White House Mess* and *No Way to Treat a First Lady*. For another humorous read, put your hands on Dave Barry's *Dave Barry Hits Below the Beltway*.

Two memoirs are musts for finding out how the powerful operate in Washington: *Personal History*, by former *Washington Post* publisher Katharine Graham, and *Washington*, by Meg Greenfield, who was a columnist and editor at the *Post* for more than 30 years before her death in 1999. *Katharine Graham's Washington* is yet another good read—an anthology of more than 100 essays and articles about Washington by an eclectic bunch of people, from Will Rogers to Henry Kissinger, compiled by Graham.

Finally, to find out more about the architecture of Washington, pick up the *AIA Guide to the Architecture of Washington, D.C.* by Christopher Weeks; for information about parks and hiking trails, look for *Natural Washington* by Richard Berman and Deborah Gerhard (I recommend these books even though both need updating).

Last but not least: The perennially inspiring words of Abraham Lincoln are always worth revisiting.

Index

See also Accommodations and Restaurant indexes, below.

United States Holocaust
    Memorial Museum, 77
Urban Chic, 92, 104, 110
U.S. Capitol Building, 17,
    28–29, 38–39
U Street Corridor/14th
    Street, neighborhood
    walk, 82–85
U Street Heritage Trail, 54

V

Van Gogh's *Self Portrait*, 62
Velázquez's *The
    Needlewoman*, 62
Verizon Center, 97
Vermeer's *Woman Holding a
    Balance*, 62
Vietnam Veterans Memorial,
    9–10
Violet Boutique, 81
Visitor information, 168
Volta Park, 118

W

Warner, John, home of
    Elizabeth Taylor and, 33
Warner Theatre, 158
Washington, George
        Gilbert Stuart portrait
        of, 57
        Mount Vernon Estate
        and Gardens, 56
Washington Monument, 10,
    40, 53–54
Washington National
    Cathedral, 21–22, 43
Washington Navy Yard, 102
Watergate Complex, 32
Weather, 178
Whistler, James McNeill, 75
White House, 31
White House Visitor Center,
    12, 31
Whitelaw Hotel, 84
Willard InterContinental, 55
Wisconsin Avenue, corner of
    M Street and, 23, 104
Wolf Trap Foundation for the
    Performing Arts, 156, 158
Woodrow Wilson House,
    52–53, 87–88
Woodward, Bob, residence
    of, 33
Woolly Mammoth Theatre
    Company, 156, 158

Accommodations

The Dupont at the Circle,
    163
The Fairmont Washington,
    162, 163
Four Points Sheraton, 163
Four Seasons Georgetown,
    162, 163
Georgetown Inn, 163
Hay-Adams, 162, 163
Hotel George, 162, 163
Hotel Helix, 162, 163–164
Hotel Lombardy, 164
Hotel Madera, 162, 164
Hotel Monaco, 162, 164–165
Hotel Palomar, 164
Hotel Rouge, 162, 164
Hotel Tabard Inn, 162, 165
The Jefferson Hotel, 165
The Liaison, 165
The Madison Hotel, 162, 165
Mandarin Oriental, 162, 165
The Mayflower Hotel,
    165–166
Ritz-Carlton Georgetown,
    162, 166
The River Inn, 166
St. Regis Hotel, 166
Topaz Hotel, 162, 166
Washington Plaza Hotel,
    162, 166
W Hotel, 166
Willard InterContinental
    Hotel, 162, 166

Restaurants

Acadiana, 135
America Eats Tavern, 135
Art and Soul, 35
Ben's Chili Bowl, 84,
    134, 135
BlackSalt, 134, 135
BLT Steak, 135
Blue Duck Tavern, 134, 135
Bourbon, 135
Bourbon Steak, 93
Brasserie Beck, 134,
    135–136
Bullfeathers, 30
Busboys and Poets, 134, 136
Café Deluxe, 22, 134, 136
Café Milano, 134, 136
Café Saint-Ex, 137
Capital Grille, 35, 134, 137
Cascade Café, 63
Cashion's Eat Place, 137
Ceiba, 137

Center Café, 42
Central Michel Richard, 137
Charlie Palmer Steak, 35
Circa, 88
Citronelle, 134, 137
CityZen, 134, 137–138
Commissary DC, 82
Daily Grill, 138
DCPieTruck, 142
The Diner, 81
Dukem Restaurant, 138
Filomena Ristorante, 24, 138
Floriana Restaurant, 138
Fogol Brothers, 142
Fossil Café, 66
Founding Farmers, 134, 138
Full Kee, 134, 138
Georgia Brown's, 138–139
Graffiato, 134, 139
Hank's Oyster Bar, 89, 139
Indique, 139
Jaleo, 139
Johnny's Half Shell, 139
Kellari, 134, 140
Komi, 140
Kramerbooks & Afterwords
    Café, 21
Lauriol Plaza, 134, 140
Martin's Tavern, 58
Matchbox, 96
Mitsitam Native Foods Café,
    78
The Occidental, 55
Old Anglers Inn, 122
PAUL, 128, 134, 140
Pavilion Café, 12, 74
Perry's, 140
Pour House, 35
Proof, 134, 141
Red Hook Lobster Truck, 142
Restaurant Nora, 134, 141
Serendipity 3, 93, 134, 141
1789, 6, 134, 141
Smith Point, 35
Sonoma Restaurant and
    Wine Bar, 18–19
The Source, 13, 141
Spy City Café, 48
Stars and Stripes Café, 71
Tabaq Bistro, 141
Tackle Box, 141–142
Teaism, 142
Ted's Bulletin, 101, 142
Tryst, 80
2 Amys, 49
Zaytinya, 134, 142

Photo **Credits**